Urban God

Urban God

JOHN PROCTOR

Bible readings and comment on living in the city

Published by
The Bible Reading Fellowship
First Floor, Elsfield Hall
15–17 Elsfield Way, Oxford OX2 8FG
ISBN 1 84101 256 4

First published 2002
10 9 8 7 6 5 4 3 2 1 0

Acknowledgments

Unless otherwise stated, scripture quotations are taken from The New Revised
Standard Version of the Bible, Anglicized Edition, copyright © 1989, 1995 by the
Division of Christian Education of the National Council of the Churches of Christ
in the USA, and are used by permission. All rights reserved.

Extracts from the Authorized Version of the Bible (The King James Bible), the
rights in which are vested in the Crown, are reproduced by permission of the
Crown's patentee, Cambridge University Press.

A catalogue record for this book is available from the British Library

Printed and bound in Great Britain by
Bookmarque, Croydon

Contents

From Bethlehem to Jerusalem

From Jerusalem to the world

Cities unseen

Final revelation

Introduction

For thousands of years people have lived in communities. Households and families have clustered into groups for company, protection and work. The biggest communities we call cities. Today's cities are often so big that they have become a web of many communities, merging and meeting, yet not quite belonging to one another. Cities can be a magnet for people from outlying regions, who move in for work and opportunity, looking for a chance to prove and improve themselves. Yet a magnet may also repel, and many city people long to be out of it, to find the release of somewhere quiet and green.

For cities are mixed places, good and bad at the same time. Much of the best of human life—technology, trade and manufacture, learning, culture and entertainment—flows out of city life. Cities bring people together. They teach us about dependence on one another. They harness human energy and strength for common purpose. Yet cities also manage to focus some of our most difficult human problems. Big cities frighten people; they seem terribly anonymous. The contrasts between wealth and poverty can be very stark. Neighbours may be many, but friends are harder to find. Crime and grime are everyday concerns. The city is always a mixed community, holding both light and shadow.

This book combs the Bible for stories about cities. The Bible speaks well of urban life, and of what it could be with God. But there is plenty of realism too, about what a mess a city can be without God. In cities, as in everything we do and everywhere we live, our human life is mixed material. We are made by God, marred by our mistakes, and yet constantly beckoned to the promise of God's renewing love. God believes in cities. But it matters too that cities believe in God.

So this book is for city Christians. Read God's story in the Bible, and hold it alongside your own. Let scripture teach you more of what God sees, enjoys and longs for in your place. And let your home city, and the witness you offer there for Christ, provide you with questions to bring to scripture. Read the Bible with sharper eyes, because the God you meet in its pages is the God you serve in the days and duties of your city life.

The book is set out in roughly Bible order, starting in Genesis, at the Tower of Babel, and running to the very end of Revelation, and God's new Jerusalem. Altogether we look at twenty scenes from the Old Testament and twenty from the New. We hear the story of Israel and her precious capital city, Jerusalem, and of the nations around that pressed and pressured her. We read of Jerusalem's ruin, of foreign exile, and of God's restoring hand that helped the Jewish people to rebuild their home. In the New Testament we track the steps of Jesus, and then follow the gospel into the cities of the Greek and Roman world in the years after Pentecost. We trace the struggles of the early Christians to sustain their faith in difficult places, and see the visions that inspired and beckoned them to the promise of God's great 'city to come'.

Throughout we listen for echoes between Bible times and city experience today. Across the centuries, from the towns and cities of the ancient world to the great communities of today, we hear of God's continuing purpose and the challenge to live by God's care.

Like many writers, I have learned an immense amount from others. I have not here acknowledged every detail of that debt. Near the end of the book, under the heading 'Further Reading', I mention a few suggestions for anyone who wants to explore the issues more fully. Books from which I have quoted are listed on a short final page headed 'Notes'. But my greater debt is to the many people I have known who live in our cities by the love and truth of Jesus Christ.

I have worked with the New Revised Standard Version, but this book can be read and used with any edition of the Bible.

First impressions

Limits to growth

Approaching any city, it is the high buildings you notice first. Tower blocks poke up into the sky. But you can only build so high. The ground conditions, building materials, technology, all limit how far we can reach. The Tower of Babel is about over-reaching. The story is not chiefly concerned with architecture or urban planning, but more with how groups of people conduct their affairs—what we aim for and why.

No one knows when or where this story was first told. It speaks of an outlook and a danger near to the heart of human nature. Yet for Jewish people in the later Old Testament period, it would have become a delightful satire, a way of thumbing their nose at the great city-power of their day. But first to the tower itself.

Pulling together

These builders appear to be organized and purposeful, people who care about shaping and conserving community. 'Let us build… otherwise we shall be scattered' (vv. 2–4). There is no dissent, no argument or half-hearted involvement. Everyone pulls together. They have the technology. This is a can-do society.

The trouble with a can-do society is that it never realizes what it can't do. It fails to see itself in any wider perspective, to look beyond its own sense of achievement and accomplishment. And eventually its only real aim will be, 'Let us make a name for ourselves' (v. 4).

The story of the Tower of Babel says that you need a better foundation than that. Technology and knowledge work best when they serve a cause beyond themselves. Even stable societies need a greater aim than mere stability. Making a name is not enough; the only name that really lasts is the name of God.

Short measure

That is the irony in this story. There is a gap between heaven and earth that all our work and wisdom cannot bridge. The people say, 'Its top shall be in the heavens' (v. 4). Then the scene switches to heaven, and God decides to come down (v. 5). The top has not met the target. Human activity has not reached high enough. And finally this pretentious project is brought to a halt, by God (v. 7), but also, we suspect, because this sort of pride is always a brittle and deceptive foundation upon which to build.

For on its own pride *deprives* us. It wraps us up in our own achievement, and makes it harder for us to receive from God. Faith and grace cannot easily meet at the top of the Tower of Babel.

Pride *deafens* us. It blocks communication and stops us hearing one another. Babel is a place where speech disintegrates. A proud person will rarely be a good listener; a proud community finds it hard to be sensitive and sympathetic.

Finally pride *divides* us. Without communication we separate. Trust erodes; care and compassion cannot flourish; people start seeking their own ends in their own ways. What Babel sets out to create, it actually destroys—the cohesion and community of human living.

If the cap fits

Six hundred years before Christ, the city of Babylon was known for its architecture. This was the high-profile skyline of the ancient east, with its ziggurats—early skyscrapers. Babylon had conquered many peoples, the Jews included, and steamrollered over their liberty and hopes. So when this story was retold by exiled Jews in Babylon, it would have brought a wry smile to hear the punch-line at the end, the first mention in the story that the place 'was called Babel' (v. 9). 'So this is what God thinks of Babylon,' hearers would say. 'It's a futile and foolish place.'

Babel is Babylon. But not just Babylon. It is any society, any community, any city that sets its own pride as the measure of its achievement.

With this story at the start of the Bible, we may fear that cities are in for rough treatment. That is not really the message. The point is that cities are deceptive. They seem to offer permanence and power, to bring people together in grand and lasting ways. But pride and appearance and 'a name' cannot really build community. Pride eventually pushes people apart, and makes communication harder. City life will never work if it is too proud, too self-sufficient, too sure of its own success—if it tries to match or copy God.

Prayer

May God help us to know our limits, and so to seek and find his love.

City salt

The long story of Abraham is not really a city tale; he is much more a nomadic and rural figure. For Abraham and Sarah, cities are stepping stones not resting places. They move out of Ur, and on from Haran (Genesis 11:31—12:4). When Abraham and his nephew Lot divide, Abraham follows a lonely route, whereas Lot goes to the cities of the valley, to the plain at the head of the Dead Sea, where there were 'great sinners against the Lord' (13:13).

We pick up the trail a few chapters later, and hear of coming disaster for the cities of Sodom and Gomorrah (18:20). Yet their sins are not spelt out in detail (except through the unpleasant story at the start of chapter 19). For the point of our passage is not city sins, but city mercies—the way in which God works even in communities that seem to be filled with faults and follies.

Countdown

The light bulb joke has brought us wit and weariness for years. 'How many... does it take to change a light bulb?' Here is a variation on the theme. How many people does it take to be the light in a community? How much righteousness makes a real difference to the atmosphere of a place? Is there a 'critical mass', a basic input of godliness, that can so affect the character of a town that the whole place looks different to God?

Abraham's prayerful countdown (vv. 22–33) puts that question to the test. What would it take for God to deal with these cities, not in ruinous judgment, but with patience and constructive purpose? The answer is that ten righteous people will do: 'For the sake of ten I will not destroy it' (v. 32).

We cannot cash that into fixed percentages. Mercy has a way of bypassing precise calculation. And in any case, we know next to nothing about Sodom and Gomorrah. Rather, this corner of scripture urges us steadily and seriously on, both to practical faithfulness and to persistent prayer.

Flavouring society

A few can make a difference. However ugly the problems and evils, the patient witness of a small group of committed people can savour a place, bringing out its goodness and limiting the effects and pace of any decay. That may be what Jesus meant by calling his friends 'salt of the earth' (Matthew 5:13). And the supreme example is Jesus himself: by that 'one man's obedience' (Romans 5:19), countless others are brought under the mercy of God.

That need not make Christian witness a comfortable thing. Goodness is not always popular: 'The drug dealers don't like us praying next to their usual place of business as it's not good for their trade,' says one church about its community outreach. There may be a cost in taking a stand. But there may be allies too.

For the text keeps saying 'righteous' (seven times in verses 23–28). In some ways righteousness has a broader reach than religion. Of course, our Christian faith should show itself in right action and in our practical contribution to society. But we may also rejoice in the meaningful goodness of neighbours, of other faiths or sometimes of none. Their contribution to the life of our cities shapes the community that God sees, affects the values and flavours the atmosphere. On some issues we shall make common cause with them, working constructively for change, glad to conserve what is wholesome, rejoicing in the signs of God's good image in people he has made.

Narrow focus, wide vision

Prayer is hard enough without having to be precise about it. Abraham's prayer shows a tenacity and an exactness that contrast with some of our customary church praying. Of course his concern is for his nephew Lot's small family. Has their influence in the city made any difference? Have they been overlooked? Is God judging too sweepingly and severely? What will become of them?

But what starts as an individual concern, driven by a family bond, becomes larger and deeper. When we care about individuals, and pray fervently for them, we are likely to find God teaching us both about communities and about himself. When we let God get involved in our love for others, we learn about God's broad and deep love for the world—for cities, for communities, and for all the people who make them what they are.

Prayer

Teach us, Lord, in expressing our love for city people, to learn more of your love.

Exodus and homecoming

Building costs

On the face of it, this is not a story about city life. It is about migrant labourers, the Hebrew people in the land of Egypt. They came as guests to find food in a time of famine. But times and personalities changed. The guests were landless folk and a potential source of cheap labour. They were also a rapidly multiplying people, altering the balance of population in the land. And when people-groups are wary of each other, one sure way to maintain distance and security is for the strong to come down hard on the people they fear.

We hear of 'supply cities' being built (Exodus 1:11), and of the endless making of bricks by gangs of workers under foremen and overseers. The scene is of messy, heavy, wearying work, with schedules dictated by the needs and plans of the masters, and a chain of authority that is quick to transmit commands from above but insensitive to legitimate complaint from below.

View from afar

So this chapter offers a distant view of city life—from below, from beforehand, from outside. Building costs. It always costs hard work and heavy effort, time and skill and care. But at its worst it can claim much more than that from the people who do it.

It can separate men from their families for long weeks and months. It can cramp workers into tight, unhealthy living conditions. It can use up a person's energy and strength too early in life, pushing for targets and finishing dates. It may—if not regulated and overseen with care—be dangerous. For building sites are dangerous places (1 Kings 16:34); and safety matters, both in the doing of the work and in the final design (Deuteronomy 22:8). And when the job is done, many of those who did it may be discarded, left to take their chance with markets and maybe moving on to new work somewhere else.

Then throughout the whole business runs the tension, between worker and final user, over cost and reward. The better the workers are paid, the more the final user will have to pay in rental or purchase price. Everyone in the chain of responsibility wants a fair share of the money, and not everyone has a strong voice to speak for their interest.

Let my people go

Here in Exodus two stories interlock. There is the particular story of a nation that God was dealing with in a special way, and preparing to be a light to all the world. This is an episode in the history of Israel. But there is also the age-old story of one group of people taking advantage of another. A proud community expands by getting others to work. This scene from Exodus has been re-run in many other places and eras.

Moses' and Aaron's 'Let my people go' (v. 1) is a first step towards escape. The Hebrew people are being led to their own land and to new hope. Their demand—to be allowed to stage a festival of faith in the desert—asserts that they belong to God, not to the religion and customs of Egypt. And that belonging will eventually lead them to freedom. But the demand to be released also comes out of God's wider care for fairness, for respect between peoples, for decent conduct in the workplace, for reasonable service and right reward. Injustice and harshness make God uncomfortable (3:9).

City questions

So one question about any grand building is, 'Who paid for this?' Not who signed the cheque, but who did the work, and what did it cost them? Were the conditions, the reward, the safety standards, the working environment, a decent and fair recognition of the job?

The flip-side of city life concerns not the public glamour and grandeur, but the ways in which the whole being of the city has been made possible and then sustained from day to day. This involves building, but also main services and transport, health and emergency cover, supplying and selling, mending and maintaining. Does the work done represent honest service, given with care, received and rewarded with respect? Do we live as community? Or do we slip too easily into working relationships marked by pressure, adversity and an endless struggle for advantage?

For thought and prayer

May God help us to value the service of neighbours,
and to seek others' good in our own work.

Safe houses

We sometimes look on cities as disorderly places, but this passage sees a very different angle—the potential for order and protection that settled and organized communities can offer to a land.

The prospect in these later chapters of the book of Joshua is Israel's new life in the Promised Land to which God has brought them. The Exodus is over; settlement and occupation have begun. The land is a good one, awash with milk and honey. But even good lands get farmed and settled by that awkward mixture of saintliness and selfishness that is human nature. Where there are people, there will be problems.

Our last reading touched on issues of safety, guarding the physical environment in which we expect people to work. This chapter too is about a safety valve for society and for its accidents, quarrels and misunderstandings.

Taking the law

The issue is accidental death—a mishap or misjudgment that costs another person's life (vv. 3–5, 9). There is no premeditated harm, no wielding of a weapon, no enmity or anger (compare Numbers 35:16–21). There may be fault, but only a careless, momentary fault; or it may be sheer accident.

Levels of fault are impossible to judge coolly and accurately in the heat of grief. We look quickly for settlement and satisfaction. In a society where murder was punished by death, and the family of the one murdered took a leading role in the punishment (see again Numbers 35), quick and rough retaliation would often seem the obvious response even to carelessness or accident. The urge to hit back might squeeze out any careful thought about rights and responsibilities.

Safe ground

That is why there were to be cities of refuge. Spaced roughly evenly across the land and accessible to any community, they provided space and safety for sudden quarrels of this kind to be sorted out (Deuteronomy 19:1–7). The person who had caused the death could run for cover and be given sanctuary by the city fathers. If the relatives of the victim gave chase, they would be stopped at the town gates; the fugitive was not for taking (v. 5).

Not that this measure was intended to provide endless safety for villains, an early version of the Costa Crime, with no possibility of extradition or accountability. There was provision for trial (vv. 6, 9), for putting the issue to the test. But trial appears to have taken place in the city of refuge, in a venue not closely linked to either family, where judges could afford to be impartial about the testimony they heard.

The years until the death of the current high priest (v. 6) were deemed to be a sufficient cooling-off period. One wonders if that would always be enough, but sometimes it would, and then the fugitive could return home with his freedom legally protected.

Just space

We have hardly any record of how well these measures worked in ancient Israel. But perhaps they have influenced our British legal habits to some degree. For people accused of serious crimes, even the remand of a prison cell may offer some safety from the rough edges of public indignation, and allow space for lawyers to gather evidence for trial. Major trials are generally held at a distance from the scene of crime, to try to prevent skewing of the verdict by strong local feeling. The public working of the law takes decisions out of the hands of victims' families. And when a person needs another chance and the opportunity to start again, moving to a big town may provide the best chance of a clean slate.

This raises again the issue of how cities can offer a true refuge, when so often they expose us to the disorder and discord that come from not knowing our neighbours. But size and anonymity can also be strengths. A big community may have the strength to absorb a quarrel, to act as arbiter, to be as fair as law can be. Then when law has done its job and levied its due, a city may offer room for a new beginning, where a person will not be known and labelled by their worst faults and follies.

For thought and prayer

Can you recall a time when you were given a new start, rather than being judged by old faults? Does anyone around you need a similar fresh beginning?

Jerusalem in the
Old Testament

2 Samuel 6:1-15, 17-19

Coming home

Many a city is seen at its brightest at carnival time. An annual festival gathers people together and lifts spirits. But the one-off celebrations—national independence, crowning a monarch, peace after war—are better and brighter still. People dance in the streets, old contacts are renewed and new friendships made. The occasion has laughter and focus, a reason for rejoicing, a sense of pleasure and plenty. A unique event will have a stamp and flavour of its own that can linger in our minds long after years of annual festivities have melted and fused into a single memory. This chapter tells of a unique moment, a day to be recalled because it could not and need not be repeated.

Capital opportunity

From one point of view this is an astute piece of political opportunism. David is Israel's king, trying to unite the nation, establish his own leadership and raise the profile of his new capital, Jerusalem. The Ark of God was the ornate wooden chest that symbolized God's presence in Israel. It spoke of preservation on the desert journey (Numbers 10:33) and of the law and love that were God's covenant gifts (Exodus 40:3, 20). To bring the Ark into Jerusalem would bind past and present, the old heritage and the new regime.

So is David just a sharp-eyed political operator, ever ready to harness religion to his party bandwagon? The chapter suggests (and Psalm 132 agrees) that he is much more—a worshipper, a man of faith and godly hope. But if he ever had any thought of cheaply adopting God for his own ends, the strange and solemn incident in verses 6–9 would have taught him a different perspective. God is not to be co-opted or taken for granted. Real holiness is a dangerous commodity.

Time for praise

The eventual arrival of the Ark is carnival indeed. There are loud music and excited voices. Crowds throng the streets to watch the procession. Food is shared among the people, and the day ends with a sense of plenty and provision, of blessing and belonging (vv. 18–19).

At the heart of all this is praise. Worship at its best is the fullest expression of joy and celebration that we can offer. The praise of this day channels elaborate ceremony and thorough preparation into a great overflow of enthusiasm and emotion. Human planning made people ready to experience the presence of God. Careful reverence led to glad rejoicing. The whole thing took time; the procession moved slowly and patiently (v. 13). Yet for many the day would have flown by: it would not have seemed slow; they would be gripped by the sense of occasion, by the sign of God's dwelling among them.

Centre to celebrate

So how can this occasion speak to the urban life of our day?

- Celebration has its place, a good place, at the heart of community life. God can enjoy a carnival and is glad to see others enjoy it too.
- God is worth celebrating. The best worship should be as good as any party, the big Christian festivals as gripping as any carnival.
- Good celebration is inclusive. People should find something in it for them (v. 19). There is plenty and pleasure, even for those on the edges of the main event.
- A city needs a sense of God at its centre. How often are new buildings called 'Centre', as if to suggest that our life revolves around the latest piece of civic or business enterprise? Yet we need deeper roots, a stronger focal point, a greater reason for praise than community life alone can provide.

Many Christians get involved in city carnivals for fun, to help the occasion along, to make it good for others. But when the litter has all been swept up, and the bunting is put away for next year, we continue to offer a solid centre point for the community. Week by week and year by year, in our Christian festivals of praise, we celebrate the coming of God—not the Ark, but Jesus. He came in human flesh to dwell among us, and in risen life to be with us for ever. These events we cannot repeat, but we can gratefully recall them, at Christmas and Easter and every Sunday. If we mark them well, we may cheerfully invite others to celebrate with us.

Prayer

May the joy of the Lord indeed be our strength, on festival days and every day.

Place for God

A city can be a symbol of something broader and deeper than its own community life. Washington stands for political power, Paris for fashion, Brussels for European union, and so on. Rome and Mecca attract pilgrims from far and wide, because each has a central role in a major world religion. So did—and does—Jerusalem.

Hub and hope

For 3000 years Jerusalem has been the great focal point for Jewish people. It is at the hub of biblical history, in Old Testament and New. This chapter continues the story of our previous reading from 2 Samuel 6, and helps to show how Jerusalem came into this role.

In 2 Samuel 6 we read of the Ark of God's covenant arriving in Jerusalem. Now we are told of a temple, built for the Ark to lodge in. Here is a 'house of the Lord' (1 Kings 6:2), a permanent dwelling-place, where God's 'name and eyes and heart' will always be present among his people (8:13; 9:3).

Solomon's temple was the first of three great temple buildings on this site. It stood from about 970 until 587BC, when Jerusalem was overrun by Babylon and many people deported. The second temple was a much plainer job, built after the exile by a dispirited nation. But it lasted for 500 years, from 515BC until Herod the Great (the angry king of Matthew 2) undertook a major remodelling and renovation. He started in 19BC, and while most of the work was done in a decade, a host of ancillary touches took until AD63 (this long process is mentioned in John 2:20). Finally, and bitterly, Herod's temple was destroyed in AD70, when the Jewish revolt was crushed by the Romans. Parts of it still remain on Jerusalem's Temple Mount.

A temple means worship. A central temple for a widely spread people invites pilgrimage, fosters a sense of devotion and indebtedness, and kindles a spirit of unity. It draws affection, footsteps and faith from far away, and makes its city into a symbol, a place of longing, loyalty and love.

Beneath the surface

So on the surface this is a grand and heartening story of a city with worship at its centre, of a nation's attention drawn to the presence of God, of political leadership inspired by praise and committed to godly ways. But there are hints that all is not well. 'Forced labour' (1 Kings 5:13–16) strikes an odd note, especially since this policy bore especially heavily on foreigners (9:20–22). The king's own palace and the house built for his bride seem as lavish as the temple itself (7:8). Where is free and faithful service, or humble leadership? Jesus said that worship and compulsion do not travel well together, nor do godly faith and harsh government (Matthew 17:24–27; 20:25–28).

Sign of glory

But the writer of 1 Kings 6 did not major on criticism. This long word-picture, this conducted tour of Israel's first temple, is intended to impress. Detail piles up, telling of peace (v. 7), purity (v. 20) and completeness (v. 22). The centrepiece is the inner sanctuary (vv. 23–28), where God's Ark is sheltered by angel wings. The whole chapter aims to remind the reader of the grandeur and glory of God, to lead us to awe and reverence, to urge us to take trouble over worship and to give God the fullest and best of our love.

A great city church may still do this. As a landmark, as a quiet refuge from busy streets, as a place hallowed by the prayers of generations, as a building serving the community yet devoted to God, it points above itself. Amid wealth it reminds us that God is worthy of lasting and lavish service. Beside poverty it represents Christ, open and merciful to all.

Of course God is not contained (8:27), and even a symbol of his presence puts responsibilities and duties upon his people (6:11–13); it's a sign of love, not a lucky charm. Yet buildings, like cities, may signal something fuller than their own life. What is built for God may beckon us to God.

Prayer

O everlasting God, in whose name are treasured here the memorials of many generations, may those who labour in this place neglect no portion of their inheritance, but guard and use it to your glory, and set forward your purpose.

A PRAYER OF J.A. ROBINSON, DEAN OF WESTMINSTER ABBEY. [1]

Solid joys

This reading and the next are psalms of praise, surely part of the worship offered by pilgrims in Jerusalem, thanking God for all that the city meant to the people of Israel. Zion (vv. 2, 11, 12) was originally a hill-fort conquered by King David (2 Samuel 5:7), which he then adopted as his capital city Jerusalem. The name Zion stuck as an alternative name for the city, and pilgrims came from far and wide to offer prayer and praise at the temple on Zion hill.

So this psalm celebrates Jerusalem as a signpost to God, a place that tells of God's greatness, where the power and permanence of heaven touch the life of earth. Zion was not the largest of mountains by any reckoning, yet the psalm praises it as 'beautiful in elevation' (v. 2). Nor was Zion in the 'far north' (v. 2) of Palestine. But some of Israel's neighbouring peoples spoke of a great mountain of the gods in distant northern parts, and the psalm adopts that way of speaking, as if to say, 'What others look for on remote hills, we have found in Jerusalem, its temple and its God. Here are fulfilled, in truth and sureness, the hopes of all the earth. God can be known here.'

Seeing and believing

Of course seeing is believing. The eye of faith finds a glory in Jerusalem that others miss. That is the point of verses 4–8. Kings came, apparently to attack the city, but could not prevail. They came, they saw, they scattered.[2] Whether this recalls a particular incident (such as that of Isaiah 36—37, see pages 34–35) we do not know. But it makes the point that real holiness deters those who do not come humbly, whereas the worshipper watches with very different eyes (v. 8). What the powers of the earth notice and what the pilgrim sees may not match, even though they look at the same thing. It was the same with the cross of Christ: some thought it a pathetic sight, while others saw the power of God in it (1 Corinthians 1:18; 2:8).

Praise, and pass it on

So verses 4–8 are the heart of the psalm, telling of the solidity of God and his city against the threatening forces of anger and chaos. On either side of this central section come two passages of praise, rejoicing in the presence, protection and permanence of God. The first runs from 'Great is the Lord' (v. 1) to 'God has shown himself a sure defence' (v. 3); and the second starts with 'We ponder your steadfast love, O God' (v. 9) up to 'let the towns of Judah rejoice because of your judgments' (v. 11).

In that last line, 'let Judah rejoice', the final intention of the psalm peeps into view. The psalmist is committed to witness, eager to let others know of the greatness of God, concerned to keep the faith by passing it on. So the final verses, 12–14, are a bridge from psalm to reader. 'You join in,' they say, as they invite the reader to tour, tell and trust, to view the city patiently and prayerfully, to trust the God who is known there, and to hand on that heritage to the coming generations.

The great Jerusalem

As this psalm stretches out to tell the generations ahead, it reaches far beyond its own time and place. For the God worshipped in Jerusalem is the God of creation, of Jesus Christ, and of final judgment and hope. Through a particular thread of history, through a single land and its people, God was preparing to reach the world with the good news of Jesus. 'Salvation is from the Jews' (John 4:22).

And so Jerusalem itself has become a symbol of something greater, of the life of heaven (Hebrews 12:22; Revelation 21:2), and of God's eternal blessing and joy. This city, with its power to inspire praise, is a foretaste, a signpost pointing to the world ahead. It speaks within time of God's sureness, splendour and strength, and of a life that transcends earth and its limits.

For heaven is a city. The Bible speaks gladly and hopefully of heaven as a big community and, despite their faults and failings, our own cities may remind us of a world to come. Crowds and company, coming together and common purpose, citadels and cathedrals, tower-blocks and trains, subways, shops and streets—all may have a voice to tell of God's coming pilgrim city, where the nations shall join in praise.

Prayer

Lord, help us to treat our cities with care and love,
to make them into places worth praising you for.

Journey's end

This is one of a sequence of psalms (120—134) labelled 'Songs of Ascents', hymns for pilgrims going up to Jerusalem. Like our previous passage, this psalm is full of confidence and gladness, in the city and in all it represents. Psalm 48 spoke of strength and sureness, of the solidity, supremacy and certainty of God, and this shorter song too rejoices in Jerusalem's firmness (122:3). But here there is a fuller note of personal warmth, of affection and love, and a more obvious emotional involvement in the good and prosperity of Jerusalem. Psalm 122 dwells less on what God has given his people, and more on what the worshipper may give to God. It is a psalm of response to grace.

Bound firmly together

Jerusalem was a point of unity for a nation, for twelve tribes spread across a broad land. Its own tightness, within a ring of walls and towers (vv. 3, 7), was a symbol of the secure relationship it offered these tribes through their common worship and faith. They came up to give thanks. As an act of obedience, they gave of themselves and their praise to God (v. 4). And as a by-product of their thanksgiving came an increased sense of belonging, of common strength, of a firm and enduring bond holding them together.

Jerusalem was Israel's centre of justice (v. 5). Part of the work of the king was judgment and the settling of laws and disputes (1 Kings 7:7). We do not know precisely how this worked, nor how the king's responsibilities meshed with more local courts and their decisions. But this psalm links unity and justice; the two must go together. A city that helps people live together fairly and truly, that sets an example of even-handed dealing and responds honestly to grievance, can be a focus of unity and loyalty for a whole land. But when the legal or administrative system of a capital city favours its own people or its own region, then it may well divide its land and erode any common commitment. (For a possible Old Testament example, see 1 Kings 12.)

Praying for peace

From justice, the psalm moves on to peace (vv. 6–9). If Jerusalem is a focus of unity, a distributor and sustainer of justice, then it matters that the city's own life be wholesome and loving. Those who love the city, who look to it and depend upon it, will also pray for it. The prayer speaks of peace 'within' (vv. 7, 8). A city's peace means much more than freedom from enemies, from danger and from outside threat. The Hebrew word is *shalom*, and it speaks of a secure, considerate and loving community life, where people can be at ease with their neighbours, themselves and their lot. True peace involves ordinary issues like friendly neighbours, safe streets, decent health care, honest business.

So the psalmist links together worship and relationships: 'For the sake of my relatives and friends, I will pray for your peace. For the sake of the house of the Lord our God, I will seek your good' (vv. 8–9). Worship brought the pilgrim to Jerusalem, and worship has created a longing for good community life. Love has led to commitment, pleasure to caring, receiving to giving.

Loyalty and love

A psalm of this kind, a 'song of Zion', speaks with many voices. In some important ways the psalmist's Jerusalem is like many another city, then and now.
- Cities may give whole lands and nations a sense of unity and focus.
- Cities have a responsibility to radiate justice, to country as well as town.
- Cities need love and loyalty, from people around as well as those within.
- We can and should pray for the peace of all our cities, for community, for care and the common good.

The peace of Jerusalem

Yet Jerusalem is unique. There is nowhere else like it. Today it is a place of reverence and devotion for three world faiths—Judaism, Christianity and Islam—and is painfully divided between Jew and Arab. The words 'pray for the peace of Jerusalem' (v. 6) sound across the centuries, and invite us to care about this place. We may not understand all the tensions, but we can pray, and can look to God to take those prayers into the tapestry of his own love for the city where he has been worshipped over so many years.

Prayer

Pray for the peace of Jerusalem.

Clean up your actions

Our last four readings, from 2 Samuel, 1 Kings and Psalms, revelled in Jerusalem's special relationship with God. As we move on to the prophecy of Isaiah, we hear a more sombre note of judgment and threat. Potential and performance do not always match; what God offers and what people make of those gifts may not correspond. But Isaiah will also have a message of hope, of promise beyond judgment and glory after sorrow.

Isaiah was a man of Jerusalem, who loved the city and understood its life. His prophecy is headed as a vision for 'Judah and Jerusalem' (1:1). Yet that very love sometimes led him to frank criticism. Isaiah desperately wanted his city to reflect the justice of God; truth, care and honesty mattered to him, and he spoke plainly about them. Many people think this first chapter is a selection of Isaiah's preaching, a summary of his message, at the head of the book.

Wasted worship

Isaiah speaks to the people of Jerusalem as if they belong to the worst communities in the world (v. 10). They have made a mockery of their special status, and their worship has become a waste. Ceremonies and sacrifices, processions and prayers—God is fed up with them all (vv. 11–15). Their worship has become meaningless and hollow, achieving nothing. In verse 15 we hear why: 'Your hands are full of blood.'

For worship is not a world of its own, not an activity we can get right in isolation from everything else we do. Because worship is open to God, it is open to the whole of life. Isaiah's challenge to Jerusalem is that worship will not move God if it does not touch the way the worshippers live. Their deeds outside the temple affect what they can offer inside. Verses 16–17 spell out that challenge in three ways.

- **Cleanse:** Isaiah tells Jerusalem to wash, to rinse the dirt and rubbish out of her life, to get rid of ways and lifestyles that are unworthy of God.
- **Change:** After the laundry, the second call is to go back to school. 'Cease

to do evil, learn to do good.' Form good habits, apply your mind, take time and effort to acquire new skills.

- **Care:** Then comes the most practical and specific challenge: 'Seek justice' (v. 17). Justice in the Bible is a very active quality. It is more than a scale sitting quietly in even balance; it is a lively commitment to correct the imbalances and unfairness of life. The downtrodden and disadvantaged, the child with no family, the home with no breadwinner—true justice notices and supports and protects. Isaiah invites his neighbours to become partners in the justice and care of God.

Choice of colours

So Jerusalem is confronted with a choice (vv. 18–20). There will be hope and prosperity if the city responds to God's challenge. They have a choice: either to live on with hands stained by the blood of their own injustice, or to seek God's forgiveness and be as clean as morning snow or new wool. They can meet God as saviour, or as judge.

For the life of the city had been rotten (vv. 21–23). People had not been truly faithful to God, but had ignored their commitment to him. Instead of justice was violence; kings were corrupt; cash, rather than care, became the great driving motive. The value and beauty God had given Jerusalem were being tainted and spoiled (v. 22).

So God speaks of judgment. He will not give up on his people. If the city will not change willingly, he will intervene to change it himself. Like fire that burns silver pure (v. 25), God will cleanse his people. Yet his aim and intention will be good and loving: to restore justice, to make Jerusalem whole again, to enable her to be truly faithful and righteous once more (v. 26).

Someone else's situation

It never does to read passages like this and think, 'It's all about someone else.' If the cap fits, we should wear it. If poor families get squeezed and the weak get hurt, if cash rather than compassion drives a city, then the call is to seek justice. God urges his people to notice their neighbours, to support the struggling, to defend the despairing, to speak for those who cannot speak for themselves. In that sense, this passage is indeed 'about someone else'.

Prayer

May God's justice live deep in our hearts, in our lives and in our cities.

Magnet for the world

Any community needs its critics, people who notice what is wrong and enable others to see it too. But we also need voices of optimism and possibility, hopeful people who see not just what is but what could be. Isaiah's prophecies to Jerusalem hold criticism and optimism in proportion, speaking frankly of sin and judgment, and boldly of the bright far horizon, of what God has yet to do.

So this reading contrasts with the solemn warnings of the last chapter. Standing alongside those words of judgment, it invites the people of Jerusalem not to fear, but to be confident and committed to God's future. If judgment comes it will be constructive and purposeful, and there will be a new dawn beyond. It is already time to live by the light of that coming day (2:5; compare Romans 13:12–13).

Far sight

Our passage matches Micah 4:1–3 almost word for word. We cannot tell which prophet first composed and spoke these stirring words. But we may at least claim for Isaiah that these lines express his vision. This is the word that Isaiah 'saw' (v. 1). Here is picture language, expressing in words what was first glimpsed in a vision or dream.

We do not fully understand how prophetic visions worked. But in Isaiah's case there may be clues in chapter 6: his calling in the temple marks him out as a man shaped by worship. Did worship, even the shallow, careless praise he attacks in 1:11–15, help him to glimpse the great purposes God was preparing for Jerusalem?

His vision is for 'days to come' (v. 2). The wording is not exact; there are no timetables. On a clear, calm day it is easier to hear faraway sounds than it is to measure the distances they travel to reach us. Isaiah is not precise, but he is clear and convinced, sharing the hope God has given him as a beacon for others to follow.

Raising hopes

Although Isaiah names no dates, the lines of his vision are strong and firm.

- **Attraction:** The vision is both national and international. The world will be drawn to Israel's God. Jerusalem will have a message for all the nations.
- **Learning:** In 1:17 Jerusalem was challenged to go back to school, to learn about goodness. Now we see Jerusalem as a schoolroom, where the whole world can learn about God's word and ways (2:3).
- **Justice:** As in Psalm 48:11 and 122:5, Jerusalem was meant to offer Israel a pattern of justice, to sustain and shape the whole life of the nation. One day that justice will reach the world: God will 'judge between the nations' (v. 4).
- **Peace:** 'Arms for farms' is the slogan in verse 4. The gentle strength of God's protecting justice will give nations the security not to fight. Then the process of learning will first involve un-learning, deliberately forgetting the arts of war, and practising a different way with neighbours. The 'peace of Jerusalem' (Psalm 122:6–9) will become peace for the world.

Vision into view

Isaiah's vision of beating weapons into ploughshares and pruning hooks has inspired many campaigners for peace. So should people of faith work to realize this vision, or simply wait until God brings it about? Perhaps we must do both —work and wait. For this vision of pilgrimage and peace will never be wholly realized by normal events of history. We cannot make the world this sort of place. For the final fulfilment of Isaiah 2 in the new Jerusalem (Revelation 21:24), we must wait on God.

Yet the stream of justice and peace going out from Jerusalem to the world has already begun to flow in Jesus. As the Christian good news goes across the earth, it beckons people to a new way of being. Jesus 'will proclaim justice to the nations' (Matthew 12:18), and bring peace to peoples long divided (Ephesians 2:14–15). So we may surely work for justice and peace as we have opportunity, in the confidence that we are swimming with the current, pursuing God's purposes, living by the light of the coming dawn. That hope can surely encourage our witness and work in the cities where we belong.

For reflection

*May God give us energy and patience to turn vision into action,
in the name of Jesus Christ. Amen.*

Enemy at the gates

Cities can be terribly vulnerable to destruction from outside or decay from within. Here, the danger comes from far away. King Sennacherib of Assyria was the great military power of the Middle East in 700BC. He boasted in his memoirs that he conquered 46 Jewish towns and shut King Hezekiah up in Jerusalem 'like a bird in a cage'. His army swept through Judah with terrible power (36:1). Despite Hezekiah's desperate attempt to buy relief (2 Kings 18:13–16), Jerusalem was placed under siege, and the Assyrian ambassadors came to negotiate terms of surrender (Isaiah 36:2–10).

What a contrast with the grand horizon of Isaiah 2! Now Jerusalem is squeezed tight by a foreign army, and the king and his advisers try to face the mismatch between the city's 'royal status and… its pitiful status'.[3] What has become of Jerusalem's special relationship with God, when it is such a minnow in world affairs?

Outside forces

Small nations still get besieged. Jerusalem in these chapters could be Sarajevo in the 1990s, hanging on in dogged determination. But even without war, cities can get badly damaged by forces from outside. A multinational firm decides to manufacture more cheaply elsewhere. A lucky break for one line of business pushes property prices out of everybody else's reach. Inter-racial or inter-religious quarrels, started long ago and far away, sour and split a local community. Drug traffickers come looking for a new market. In a hundred ways a city's life can come under assault. History and heritage, all the bonds and values that have held the community together, suddenly seem terribly fragile. The new voices are seductive and almost convincing: 'We have the power. In fact we even have God on our side' (36:10).

Resources for survival

In chapter 36 the siege is laid. In chapter 37 the situation is resolved. There is no great fight-back, no inventive military manoeuvre, no ambush or decoy.

The Bible often honours human skill and courage, but here the weapons and tactics are those of faith (compare 2 Corinthians 10:4). Prophecy, providence and prayer are the three main ingredients.

- Prophecy comes first. Isaiah speaks a word from God (37:5–7). He has the calm, the faith and the openness to God to see beyond the immediate crisis and to give confidence to others. He interprets the mind of God for the situation and the moment.
- God gets involved. Of course God is constantly involved, but not always in ways we can trace or foresee. Providence is God's purposeful love, wisely guiding and directing the events of earth. The prophesied rumour has the desired effect (37:7–9), and the Assyrian king moves off, shaking his fist and promising to return (37:10–13).
- King Hezekiah prays (37:14–15). As Isaiah himself had experienced (Isaiah 6), the temple seems to give the king a different perspective on the power structures of the world. God is supreme over all rulers and nations, and it matters that people know that (37:16–20).

Facing danger

Jerusalem did not have a charmed life; she had a covenant life, founded on a two-way relationship with God. She had no right to take God for granted; but she was called to trust him. These chapters still offer guidance and wisdom to Christians as we try to sustain the life of our communities.

- Prayer is vital. It teaches us to see with new eyes, to look above the immediate danger and into the presence of God.
- Prophecy is the gift of speaking God's word into a difficult situation, whether to stir or to steady. The person who can say with authority, 'Do not be afraid' (37:6) will give others space and stimulus to renew their faith and to form fresh resolve.
- Providence has no fixed patterns, except that we should expect surprises. When God is at work, the last find their way to the head of the queue, and the strong are liable to stumble. For God, the ultimate power is not in military strength, nor in malice, nor even in market forces. It is in the meekness and mystery that we see most clearly in Jesus Christ.

For prayer

*Pray for perspective and protection, and for a clearer view of
God's purpose and power in your community.*

A world out there

Changing minds

Only Jonah, of all the Hebrew prophets, is sent to speak to a foreign people. His story takes us (by the oddest of routes) far away from Israel, hundreds of miles to the north-east, to Nineveh in present-day northern Iraq. Nineveh was the capital of the Assyrian empire, and the Jews knew of it by repute and experience. For Assyria was a great power in her time, and a thorn in the side of her weaker neighbours (see, for example, 2 Kings 18:9–11; or our last reading, Isaiah 36 and 37). So far as the Jews were concerned, Nineveh was a vicious and ungodly place. Jonah's mission, says one writer, is like sending a mouse to preach to cats.[4]

Hard to swallow

Modern readers may find parts of Jonah's story hard to swallow, but the point the writer really wanted the readers to digest is this: God loves Nineveh, and he sees hopes and possibilities in Nineveh that Jonah cannot or will not see. God's vision is broader, God's love is deeper, God's compassion beats more strongly than Jonah can easily understand or share. God has more faith in the city than Jonah does.

Jonah's about-turn, his journey west when God sent him east (1:2–3), is explained at the end of the book (4:2). He was not afraid of failure. But he was afraid of success—fearful that Nineveh would actually listen to his message. As a member of the family of faith, as an Israelite, he found it terribly hard to believe that God could love an alien, pagan, evil people like the Ninevites. And if God did love them, that was God's business. He, Jonah, wanted no part of it.

New thoughts

Eventually, Jonah does obey (3:3), and his worst fears are realized. People heed his message, and from then on the story is all about the changing of minds and hearts. The people of Nineveh change their minds, and turn to God (3:5–9). God appears to change his mind too, switching his attitude from judgment to mercy (3:10). That was the plan all along, but the story tells it here as God's response to human repentance and faith, his coming to meet the people who are turning to him.

This leaves only one mind to be changed—Jonah's. The whole of chapter 4 is about God wrestling with Jonah to lead him to a more open, patient and generous faith. At first Jonah is miserable and resentful (4:1–3). And even at the end, there is only a question mark (4:11). Like the prodigal's elder brother (Luke 15:25–32), we never find out for sure how Jonah responds. Has he come to share God's love for Nineveh, or not? That is left as a question for the reader too. Not just, 'What did Jonah decide?' but also, 'Where do you stand?'

Filleting out a message

What sort of writing is the book of Jonah? Did it really happen exactly as told, or was it always intended as an extravagant story? Commentators disagree, but the message of the book of Jonah is very clear.

- Jonah challenges God's people to let the great evils of the world shape our mission.[5] Where needs and hurts are sharpest is a place for Christ to be named and his love shared.
- Jonah speaks of a big movement of repentance and faith, of people turning to God, not in a trickle but in a torrent. Even in days of struggle, we may long and pray for the swift expansion of God's kingdom.
- Jonah shakes us out of any thought that God's horizons are as narrow as ours. A church that is successful in mission will not remain the same, filled with all the same sort of people as before. Good mission will change our churches and challenge our thinking.
- Jonah teaches us that God can use even blinkered people, like ourselves, to serve his cause. But we shall love better if we are also prepared to learn.
- Finally, Jonah is a sign (Matthew 12:40–41). God is never defeated. Christ is risen. Whatever people may do to quench and suppress them, God's truth and love run on.

Prayer

May God help us not to be swallowed by fear, but to serve in faith.

Star quality

Prophets to the world

Several of the Old Testament prophets spoke the judgment of God against foreign nations and powers. They believed that the God of Israel was God of the whole world. When Jewish people were drawn into the quarrels, wars and pressures of international life, it mattered to know that God was still at work. The whole of creation remains under his eye and love. Though the world may not realize it, the nations are measured by his justice.

This reading is a 'taunt against the king of Babylon' (v. 4). But which king does it mean? A recent and responsible suggestion[6] links this poem to the passing of King Sargon, who died in 705BC on military campaign (see v. 19). Sargon governed the Assyrian empire (see our last reading), and his lands included Babylon, which was then a city-state in present-day southern Iraq. Carvings and inscriptions of the time show him as a harsh and aggressive ruler.

Return to quiet

Isaiah's poem does not describe precisely how the king falls, but it sketches the effect of his demise in a series of pictures, and gradually we realize the impact that this reign has had on other lands around.

- **Staff shortage (vv. 5–6):** A broken royal sceptre is like a torn and muddied flag. It is a symbol of control ended and power that has disappeared. This has been an ugly power, and the ending of tumult and torture brings a deep rest to the nations.
- **Peace on earth (vv. 7–8):** Even the trees in Lebanon feel relief and ease. This may mean the sigh of subject peoples, relieved to be free from oppression. But it also hints at the way proud cities will plunder every available natural resource, with an unseeing disregard for any consequences. Even in the ancient world, some prestigious building projects stripped whole lands of decent timber.

- **Shadows and stars (vv. 9–17):** In the world of the dead, the ghosts of earth's great rulers stand amazed at this new addition to their company. Babylon was the home of astronomy, and her king felt like a star himself, a man raised far above the ordinary levels of earth. But eventually all his sparkle passes into the half-light of death and decay. Despite his power, and the breadth and brutality of his rule, he is ultimately as weak as anyone else, levelled and lowered from the skies into the shades.
- **Memory blank (vv. 18–21):** And what is left behind? A noble memory? No, just a record of shameful deeds. This is a man who will not be remembered in an elaborate ceremony or an ornate tomb. And he does not deserve any memorial. His life is better forgotten.

Eternal city

Though the king was dead, Assyria (and later Babylon) would remain a force in the world, and both would deal brutally and bitterly with the Jewish people. Indeed, many scholars believe that Isaiah's words here found new and fresh relevance in the sixth century BC, when the Jews suffered under Babylon's rule.

But the force of these verses reaches further still, to challenge tyranny and arrogance in every age and place. For even though Babylon was eventually completely snuffed out, her name endured as a byword for greedy pride. For example, in the book of Revelation, 800 years after Isaiah, Babylon is a code name for the self-importance and avarice of the Roman empire. Another instance comes from much nearer our own day. As the Second World War ended in 1945, German theologian Gerhard Ebeling sat among a group of weary soldiers and read to them Isaiah 14, from verse 12. For him, the tumbling star, the king whose fall released the world to peace, was Hitler.

There are Babylons in every age. For Babylon is any great power or city that imposes its personality on distant peoples, that ravages the earth to satisfy its own pleasures, whose leaders think too highly of their role in the world. Yet death sweeps everything away, and the deceits and destructions of Babylon will be better forgotten than remembered.

Many Christians live in Babylon—or at least in cities and societies that have something of Babylon about them. How can we act with integrity? Our next reading offers some guidance.

For prayer

Pray for leaders of the nations, that their rule may not hurt or harm God's world.

Seek the welfare

Home discomforts

For many in our world, exile is a fact of life. They have fled from war or poverty or fear, and the only home they have is a foreign land, with no clear prospect of ever going back. The great cities of the world are full of exiles—people caught between two networks of language, custom and culture, stranded between memories and hopes.

For others in the city, exile is a symbol of how life has come to feel. They may appear at home and secure in their own land, but times and communities can change. When the things dearest to you matter little to your neighbours, it is hard to feel truly at peace.

Many people of faith are ill-at-ease in the modern secular city. When the community's rhythms and routines, its values and its visions, are at odds with those we trust and treasure, there is a sense of alienation, of not really belonging. So how can you cope, and how do you contribute, when you are not quite at home? We listen in this reading to the Jewish people's experience of exile in Babylon in the sixth century BC.

Letter from home

Jeremiah writes in about 594BC. Babylon, the great power of the day, had overrun Jerusalem in 597, installed a puppet king, and deported many of the most gifted and influential people. This is a pastoral letter, offering a word from God to the elders of the exile community. The message is positive, but surely not what many of them wished to hear.

Jeremiah speaks of God's concern for their 'welfare' (v. 11); the Hebrew word is *shalom*, 'peace'. One day God will bring his people back home (vv. 10, 14). But they will only discover their true *shalom* from God if they first seek the *shalom* of the city where they now live (v. 7). Amid the evils of exile they must turn the situation to good. For all the temptation to look back and live in the past, they must face and shape the present and the future.

'Settle' is the word. Quite literally, dig in (v. 5). Do not trust easy promises (vv. 8–9); there will be no quick fix. But raise families, and look forward (v. 6). Exile is the present reality, so come to terms with it. Only by living positively through the present days will the exile people find strength to believe and hope in God's future purpose.

Seventy years (v. 10) is a lifetime. The men and women who went into exile will die there. But only if they can nurture their hope will there be children and grandchildren who will want to return. The exile people are God's key to Israel's future (vv. 11–14). It is their faith and prayer that will sustain the nation's spirit. In the misery of exile, God is trusting them to keep alive their love for him, for the sake of generations to come.

Home-making

Exiles for God have to be committed to the present. Only so shall we see clearly that God is Lord of all time, of the future as surely as the past. Only so shall we have a distinctive contribution to make. Only so can we keep hope alive of a God who transforms every present and every place.

Christians often lament our status in the secular city. It does not dance to our tune or value what we hold dear. We do not determine its life, nor does it rate us highly as an influential people. But we need not retreat. The *shalom* of the city is our business, and only through caring about that will we discover any *shalom* of our own. This involves neighbour love, putting down roots, and getting dirt under our fingernails.

That sort of commitment can kindle hope, and hope in return gives energy, grip and generosity to today's service. Commitment and hope can be passed on to a new generation. Nostalgia cannot.

Seventy years was roughly the length of the Jewish exile in Babylon (v. 10). It was roughly the length of time that Christian witness was suppressed in communist Eastern Europe. If the Church in the West senses the tide going out, we may need to be ready for the long haul, to love the communities where God has put us now, and so to hope for the day when our cities will find their true *shalom* in the peace of Jesus Christ.

For reflection

What can you do for the welfare of the city where you live, starting where you are?

Pride comes before...

Tyre was a city with attitude. It was proud of its success and its security, and considered itself superior to other places and powers around. It was a port, 100 miles north of Jerusalem, on the Mediterranean coast of Phoenicia (modern Lebanon). Part of the city was a small offshore island and part was on the mainland; the two were linked with a causeway.

Tyre was the great middle-man of the ancient Middle East. The harbours were busy, ships plied to the coasts and islands of the Mediterranean, and there were well-organized networks of land transport reaching far into the rich territories of the east and south. Tyre accrued and acquired very nicely, by its natural harbour, its favourable site and, above all, by its trade.

Trade and tragedy

Tyre had been on good terms with Israel's early kings, David and Solomon (2 Samuel 5:11; 1 Kings 5:1–12). But this passage from Ezekiel comes from 400 years later, in 586BC, at a miserable time in Jewish history. Jerusalem had fallen to Babylon, the rising power of the day. And what did Tyre do? She laughed.

For Tyre felt like a queen. If a foreign army was in the area, she could simply retreat to her island, put up the shutters and sit tight. More importantly, if Jerusalem had fallen, Tyre would have some extra business. 'I shall be replenished' (v. 2). One person's disaster is another person's dividend. Share prices in Tyre would rise, there would be a buzz around the quays and warehouses, money would be spent in the shops and bars, and merchant families would be able to extend and improve their homes. The mood of the moment was of comfort, confidence and complacency. But, says Ezekiel, the moment will not last.

The next domino

This prophecy against Tyre goes on for three chapters. Chapter 26 talks of power, 27 of possessions, and 28 of pride. The burden of this first chapter is that Tyre will fall, just as Jerusalem has fallen. If one domino in a line topples over, the next will soon tumble too. There will be a grim siege (26:7–12), and Babylon will have the power and patience to grind Tyre into submission.

In fact the island of Tyre did not come to ruin in this period; it was not reduced to a fish dock (vv. 5, 14) just yet. But Babylon did destroy the mainland side of Tyre, and appoint its own governor for this island port. Tyre did not prosper from its apparent window of opportunity.

For whom the bell tolls

The mood of this reading may seem vindictive. But part at least of the chapter invites a very different response. The 'princes of the sea' (other ports) raise a lament (26:15–18). When Tyre falls, they tremble too. They do what Tyre would not do for Jerusalem: they mourn. They feel their own vulnerability. When destruction is in the air, none of us gains anything from the ruin of a neighbour.

Despite her selfishness, there is sorrow in the wreck of the great ship Tyre (27:26). Her goods, her friends, her contacts will all go under with her (27:33–35). Despite all her arrogance and pride (28:2), her humbling is as deep a misery as the driving of Adam and Eve from the garden (28:11–19).

For no one, not even Tyre, is an island. We are mortal together. One person's wounds are my weakness. A neighbour's humiliation should humble me too. Another's disaster is cause for my distress. The funeral bell robs us all of a part of life. There is no other way to be truly human.

But for Tyre, and for any community that is driven by business and balance sheet alone, it is hard to think humanly. The bottom line gets in the way. A neighbour's grief may turn out for my gain. One firm's redundancies may be another's overtime. Your shipwreck may help my shares.

So Tyre speaks to every finance-driven city, reminding us not to be driven right away from our humanity. For all our money, we are mortal, fragile and vulnerable. We do well to remember how to weep, how to feel for a neighbour, how to hurt for another's wounds, how to speak in days of sorrow. For one day all our gold will be dust, and the only commodity that holds its value for ever will be love.

For prayer

Pray for people who work with money, that they may see wider issues, seek the common good, and serve their neighbours honestly and fairly.

Destruction and hope

Weeping with God

Our last reading mentioned, as if from afar, the terrible destruction of Jerusalem by the armies of Babylon in 587BC. Judah's puppet king rebelled, and his masters crushed him. Our remaining five Old Testament readings reflect this event and the Jewish people's attempts to recover. Three are passages of hope and reconstruction; but first come two poems of the sharpest and most bitter sorrow.

Here in Lamentations are some of the Bible's most desperate and miserable prayers. Yet the book is not a careless composition. Each of the first four chapters is an acrostic: the 22 lines begin with the letters of the Hebrew alphabet, in sequence. Into a patient, structured, deliberate piece of poetry are distilled the hurts of a broken city.

Grief in the city

For me, Lamentations draws attention not just to its own city, but to the areas and lives in every city that are troubled, bruised and neglected. The language of broken buildings, hungry children and wasted potential speaks of the old lady whose life is made a misery by vandalism, the homeless teenager scavenging in litter bins, the home where long-term unemployment has sapped self-respect. It invites me to pray for children playing among broken glass in the park, for teenagers damaged by drugs, for parents strained to the limit of their endurance and love, for old people who find the world a lonely and inhospitable place.

Of course these were not the exact issues faced by the biblical poet. He wrote about his home and his own grief. But his God is ours too, and this whole world is God's. So we may rightly weep with Lamentations for the ancient sorrow of Jerusalem. And Lamentations will weep with us for the sorrows we see, and the hurts we bear and share.

Jerusalem, Jerusalem

Here are towns and buildings destroyed (vv. 2, 5), and a people hungry and sick (vv. 11–12, 19–20). Strong young people have been killed (v. 21), along with leaders of stature and experience (v. 20). Beauty has turned to dust (vv. 15–17), dignity to despair (v. 10), security and leadership to rudderless and meaningless drift (v. 9). The people live like slaves (5:2–5, 13), amid violence (5:9, 11), famine (5:10) and ruin (5:18).

On the whole canvas of world history, the sack of Jerusalem is one destruction among many. But Lamentations draws the reader in, so that the stench and sorrow surround us, and we feel, in even a small way, how absolute and complete a misery this is for those caught within it. This is the tragedy of a city become a wilderness, with a past but no clear future, levelled by hate, and loved with an utterly helpless love. Yet even this helplessness may be brought to God.

Look, Lord

Lamentations 2 speaks of the disaster as the work of God: 'The Lord has done it' comes over and again through verses 1–9. This is partly a wrestling with Israel's special relationship to God. But it is more: it is an acknowledgment of God's responsibility, an awareness that God is the only one who can redeem and turn back the situation.

Then at the heart of the chapter is the poet's own pain. 'How can I comfort you?' (v. 13). This is first-person sorrow, the love of one who can say, 'My eyes… my stomach… my bile' (v. 11), bringing to God the hurts of his community and his own care.

Finally comes a desperate appeal to God (vv. 18–22). 'Weep ceaselessly. Lift your heart and hands. Tell him what we are going through.' Prayer does not try to explain suffering; it expresses it. Prayer may bring to God the things we do not understand and the feelings we cannot censor. Prayer wants God to hurt too, to weep with us and feel with us, to know the weakness of our flesh and to share our brokenness.

When we pray about the destructions and distresses that truly grieve us, our language will not be tidy or precise. Lamentations allows—invites, warrants, maybe even requires—that untidiness. When the griefs of the city claim and strain our energies and emotions, we may involve God to the same extent that we are involved, and lay hold on God in passionate and compassionate prayer. For this is the God of Passion—and of resurrection too.

For reflection and prayer

Weep with those who weep (Romans 12:15).

Rise up, O God

So far as we can tell, this desolate psalm comes from the same time as Lamentations, in the years after the destruction of Jerusalem in 587BC. The atmosphere is broadly similar to our last reading: the gloomy moods of the two passages match quite closely. But not exactly.

This psalm is more dynamic in the way it lays hold of the grace and love of God. Lamentations surveyed the hurt of the city, and took to God its helpless sorrow and pain in an almost passive, numb prayer. Psalm 74 has a much clearer demand that God should act, that his record, his relationship with Israel, and indeed his own reputation require him to stir and to save.

We need both aspects in our prayers. Lament, for the question without an answer and the hurt without any sign of healing, is a proper part of biblical praying. When life is filled with distress and disorder and destruction, then we may rightly pour out tears of misery and sorrow before the face of God. But faith, active and persistent faith, nourishes itself not only on grief but also on memories of grace. There is a time for speaking before God the convictions and concerns that have sustained us in the past, for asking God sharp questions, and for urging God to act.

Questions and memories

The start of this psalm goes directly to the heart of the matter with an agonized question: what has gone wrong, that God has led Jerusalem into such utter desolation (v. 1)? Does he not remember that these are his people, loved and cherished from long ago (v. 2)? Will he not come and see what has happened to them (v. 3)?

Verses 4–9 recall the dreadful days when enemy soldiers wrecked the temple, destroying the silence (v. 4), the splendour (vv. 5–6) and the sanctity (v. 7). Now there is no meeting place for God's people (v. 8), and no leaders to see beyond the present troubles (v. 9). There is only a dreadful vacuum, and a horrid quiet—as if God has opted out or is not there at all. Will it ever end (vv. 10–11)?

Towards hope

The first steps towards hope come by remembering God's creation. The natural world is full of nourishment, love, provision and order (vv. 12–17). In creation God has brought purpose in place of chaos, life instead of destruction. If God can do that for the world, can he not do it again for his own people? Will he not remember (v. 18)?

So the psalm ends with 'remember… regard… rise up' (vv. 18, 20, 22), and with one final 'remember' (v. 22). Out of this appeal to God will come watchful trust, to look for the first opportunities for revival and restoration. The waiting will be long, and the days slow and hard, but God has not forgotten, and nor has Israel's faith.

Tales of our time

Many Christians from across the world have visited the vast roofless shell of the old Coventry Cathedral in the English Midlands, destroyed with much of the medieval city by German bombs in the Second World War. On that site, which remains a place of Christian worship, just across from the modern cathedral, is a centre for reconciliation, teaching the arts of peace and international friendship, building relationships and hope among the broken stones.

A city church was burned one night, so badly that it could never be used again. Members of the congregation gathered outside the next Sunday morning, and sang, 'O Jesus, I have promised to serve thee to the end.' Nearly 20 years on, the national press recently reported the caring work being done by that congregation, with a new and smaller building, amid severe social problems in the area.

For faith in the city believes that, with God, destruction need never be the last word. There are many reasons for that faith. Coventry Christians drew on their trust in Jesus as Prince of Peace. The burned-out congregation sang of his enduring presence and friendship. Psalm 74 turns to God's creative power and love, as the first step back to hope. Faith may question, but it need not quit, even when it can neither explain the past nor understand the present.

For reflection

Experience is the clay that faith moulds into prayer. Faith does not deny experience, but shapes it into an appeal to God.[7]

Fresh possibilities

Ezekiel was an exile prophet. He was among the Jews, deported to Babylon in 597BC, who heard ten years later of the final ruin of Jerusalem. As he wrestled, from far outside the Promised Land, with his own hopes and doubts, he tried to strengthen the faith of his fellow exiles. But his sights remained firmly fixed on home, and the climax of this book (chs. 40—48) is a long and complex prophecy of Jerusalem coming back to life. More particularly, Ezekiel's vision is of Jerusalem renewed at its very centre, of a rebuilt temple and restored worship. Here, in chapter 47, we are led away from the temple courts themselves, along the river of God.

Stream of life

The river comes from the very centre of the new temple, as if there is a spring in the rock beneath. It runs across the enclosed courts and trickles out beside the east gate, like water glugging out of a bottle. Through this east gate God came to dwell in the temple (43:1–5), just as in an earlier vision God's glory had left the city and moved east (10:19; 11:23). Now God has returned, and his return has brought life.

Water supply is still a contentious issue in the Middle East. In a hot, dry climate, water is absolutely vital for a land to flourish. But in Ezekiel's vision water is not a scarce resource; it is a generous and ample gift. Mysteriously, miraculously, the stream gets deeper as it runs, from trickle to ankle-deep, from knee-high to waist-high, and eventually a full river, too deep to ford (v. 5).

The river runs down to the Dead Sea (as we call it), the lowest spot on earth, an inland sea many times saltier than the ocean. And the fresh water sweetens the dead, salty places. Fish return, and the waters teem with life. Trees grow along the river (vv. 7, 12), bursting with fruit and wholesome to heal. The whole picture is of life restored and a land released, in place of desert, dryness and death.

From past to future

Biblical scholars have traced the currents of tradition that run through this scripture: of Jerusalem as a city nourished by fresh streams (Psalm 46:4), and of the rivers in the Garden of Eden (Genesis 2:10–14). Ezekiel's vision seems to mingle these images, portraying Jerusalem as a city nourished by God so that she can renew creation and give life to dry earth. Jerusalem had seemed an exhausted city, drained of all life and hope; now she can start to give again. From a new temple and restored worship comes fresh life for a weary land.

Wealth to share

This is our third reading about the ruin and reconstruction of Jerusalem, and the first in which hope has been the dominant theme. Ezekiel's vision may never have been intended as a literal and exact map of how things would be. Yet it is powerful and subtle, a picture of hope, a signpost to beckon people forward. The vision spoke for a miserable and troubled city, not just of recovery, but of what Jerusalem could give and share with the land around. This would be a generous city, enriching many through God's goodness. Cities were never meant to be self-centred; at their best they can shape a wide land for good and for God. A city with hope can give opportunities for work and learning, facilities and markets, wisdom and wealth, a sense of optimism, activity and promise.

Creation and Christ

The emphasis on creation may seem strange. It figured in our last reading from Psalm 74, and comes again here in Ezekiel. What, we may wonder, have cities to do with creation, concrete with crops, and buildings with natural beauty? Yet scripture reminds us, even in the heart of the city, not to forget the variety and splendour of God's creative love. For a Christian, nature is nurture: remembering God's creative work can kindle our faith and refresh tired spirits, just like a river in the desert. Finally, and much later, we see Jesus drawing on this same image of Jerusalem as a great spring, as if to say, 'I am God's new temple. From me rivers of life-giving water will flow to the world' (John 7:37–39).

For reflection

For Ezekiel, as in so many other places in the Bible, worship is vital. Renewal comes from the temple. Proper praise transforms a place. How can the worship and prayer of your church nourish your local community?

New world coming

Israel's exile eventually ended. The people who returned, and some who had stayed through the bitter years, began to rebuild their world. These were hard days in Jerusalem; progress was slow and problems were many. Colonial masters kept a watchful eye on developments. Foreign neighbours took a jealous interest. A society cannot settle quickly when it has been unsettled so severely. Rights and duties, structures of care and support, patterns of worship, all took time to form. Families worked to set up homes and grow food. Some people were good at looking out for their own interests, but slower to spot the need and weakness of others.

The last portion of Isaiah, chapters 56—66, speaks a word from God to this situation. There is a sense of the struggle, challenge and confusion many in Jerusalem were facing. Yet near the end of the book comes a bright vision of what could be and what God will do. As people hold on in faithfulness, the world will change.

Home truths

Our reading begins with a large horizon: 'new heavens and a new earth' (v. 17). It ends with a picture of nature transformed (v. 25), and a glimpse of unimaginable harmony and hope, where predators sit quietly alongside their one-time prey, and even the lion is a vegetarian! The message is, 'Think big, think broad, think beyond what you see, think believingly of a God whose purpose is wider and more generous than you can imagine.' God can refashion the world in ways his people would never guess. And this God has a purpose for Jerusalem.

For sandwiched between the big horizons is a local, practical vision for Jerusalem and its life (vv. 18–23). The God of big plans and wide purpose knows the daily pressures and burdens of the city. God understands power and poverty, illness and insecurity, work and wealth, weariness and weakness. This local vision speaks of security from distress, of protection for the young and welfare for the old, of food and shelter, and of fair reward for hard work.

Isaiah vision

A fascinating little book by Raymond Fung[8] adopts these verses as a guide for Christian witness in the world today. For here, he argues, are four prime values:

- Children should not die, and parents should not fear for their children's welfare (vv. 20, 23).
- Old people matter. They should be accorded nurture and dignity through their later years (v. 20).
- People should be able to make decent homes, and to live safely and confidently in them (vv. 21–22).
- Food is vital. Its steady and sure supply is basic to human welfare. People should be able to secure this, without fear of losing it (vv. 21–22).

If Christians will work for these values, says Fung, our local communities will change. We shall build bridges to the concerns and needs of our neighbours, and many will discover through us the wisdom and care of God. Child health, respect for old age, housing, hunger—if these issues stir us, then our action will be both biblical and relevant, and will make the gospel known with fresh and compelling power.

Rainbow journey

The big vision—like that first covenant sign, the rainbow—is always ahead of us. Only in God's final coming city will the new heaven and new earth fill every horizon (Revelation 21:1). Yet the big vision is vital, for within it we shall see every step as part of a journey, every small gain as part of a greater gift, every glimmer of light as a foretaste of dawn. The big vision gives stamina and energy for the present struggle.

For the world's carnivores—animal and human—still prowl and prey on the weak. But God's people may act to protect the vulnerable, to honour neighbours' work, to guard and cherish community bonds, in the confidence that God is on our side. God is working through and above and beyond all our efforts, towards the full and final coming of new heavens and a new earth.

Prayer

Teach your Church, Lord, to be long-sighted, to see the far vision,
so that today's work may serve your wider purpose of welfare and love.

Rise up and build

Nehemiah was a spiritual person, but he was a very practical person too. In this book prayer and action go together. So do strong, clear-headed leadership and willing teamwork. Love for Jerusalem leads its people into the hard work of reconstruction. Here are dust and grit, hard labour and heavy lifting, skilful workers and sceptical neighbours, long days of patient progress, and eventual success.

The year is 445BC. The first wave of returning Jewish exiles reached Jerusalem nearly 100 years earlier, but rebuilding the city had been a desperately slow business. Indeed, a recent attempt to repair the walls had been thwarted and abandoned (Ezra 4:7–23). Nehemiah was disturbed by the news he heard (1:1–3), and asked permission to leave his comfortable job with the Persian king, and go to Jerusalem to tackle the situation (1:11—2:8).

Night rider

The main point of the secret foray (vv. 11–15) is to gain information about the state of the wall. Part of it was just a heap of rubble (v. 14). The lowest part of the wall, at the south-east corner of Jerusalem, had run across a steep hillside. Now there was only 'a vast tumble of stones',[9] the debris of collapsed terraces. It seems from the list of landmarks in chapter 3 that Nehemiah decided instead to reinforce a much older wall, on top of the ridge.

Good information leads to sensible planning. But good local knowledge does more than this, in any piece of community action. It gives the conviction and the credibility to lead. Nehemiah wants to encourage and organize others in the repair work. He will only be able to do that if he knows what he is talking about. And now he does.

Joining in

The people in Jerusalem are quick to follow Nehemiah's invitation, and the work is put under way. His leadership moves and motivates. What is the secret of his success?

- **Prayer:** Nehemiah knows God, and has developed his plans in conversation with God (1:4–11).
- **Politics:** The project has proper permissions and backing from the due authorities (2:1–9).
- **Practicality:** Nehemiah has checked out the most difficult part of the job, and has thought about materials, too (2:8).
- **Personal integrity:** When a leader really cares about the task, everybody notices. Commitment carries conviction.
- **Pride:** Nehemiah offers the people the proper pride of a job well done. The 'disgrace' (2:17) of ruin and rubble will end.

Leading spirit

When cities get run down, so that communities start to lose their pride and spirit, a person like Nehemiah can make an immense difference. A good Nehemiah needs many qualities: a sharp eye for the gifts and graces God puts in other people's lives; courage and stamina; infectious commitment; the ability to face difficulties and disagreements. And so often these qualities are rooted in a secure and deep relationship with God. Prayer and faith give the confidence to keep going, to inspire others, to handle discouragement, to turn vision into reality.

One of the finest Christian initiatives I have seen in an inner city uses a motto from this chapter: 'Let us rise up and build' (v. 18, AV). The people in that place have been building for many years. But bricks and mortar have only been incidental. The real building is in human lives, mostly young lives. The materials have been care and compassion, patience and determination, laughter and sorrow, local knowledge and the love of Christ. The whole work and its values are rooted in the Christian gospel. No one has ever hidden the fact that this is a church project, though that has been costly at times. And by the grace of God, the vision has become reality, year after year and decade after decade.

For reflection

Do you take a balanced approach to your responsibilities—both prayerful and practical? On which side are you stronger—prayer or practical action? Should you try to strengthen the other side of your service? Or is it sufficient to rely on the contribution of others?

From Bethlehem
to Jerusalem

Royal cities

As we launch into the New Testament, the Bible's story has moved on through more than 400 years since the time of our last reading in Nehemiah. The fortunes of the Jewish people have risen and fallen, and once again they have become a subject people. In this era the major player is the city of Rome. Her territory runs around the Mediterranean, and Palestine is just a remote strip of land, squeezed between the sea and the eastern boundary of empire.

People who count

Rome is not mentioned in this reading. It does not need to be. When 'a decree went out from Emperor Augustus' (v. 1), everyone knew this was an act of Roman power. This was not a single, instant census, as happens today, but a patient and cumulative survey of the empire's resources. The issue was tax, so this was a 'registration' (v. 2) of population, of property, and of the land's productivity. Poll tax and property taxes were reckoned with care.

The whole exercise sets Palestine's status in perspective. The network of provincial government extends the reach of Roman imperial power far across the world. Within this system, Palestine is reckoned as part of Syria (v. 2). She has a client king of her own—Herod, who is answerable to Rome—but in administrative terms she is merely a sub-district of a distant province.

Two kingdoms

Joseph probably journeyed to Bethlehem because of property holdings. If he had ancestral roots and a share in family land at Bethlehem, he would be expected to acknowledge responsibility for it. So a second royal city, beside Rome, comes into Luke's picture. For Bethlehem had been the home of King David. And suddenly this gospel account has become a tale of two kingdoms.

Out of David's line a new kingdom is coming. In a royal household long defunct, God is raising a new leader (1:32–33). From beneath the heavy restraints of Roman authority, green shoots of hope poke through. But the two kingdoms will contrast sharply. Rome reaches out with force and law, to grasp and to gain. Jesus will offer his own weakness, and will give himself.

Bethlehem, 'royal David's city', was really just a small town. But as this gospel begins with a Roman decree, summoning Joseph to Bethlehem, so Luke's story ends with a different message running right back to Rome (Acts 28:31). Followers of Jesus announce, in the very centre of empire, the kingdom that comes from Bethlehem, and its Prince of Peace, Jesus Christ.

Two kinds of power

So here are two sources of power, and two kinds of power. Rome held the power of politics, firm government and military might, of financial planning and tight control. Here was a great imperial city, concentrating wealth, ruling firmly, claiming the loyalty of subject peoples, but in an unequal relationship where all the pride and prestige gravitated towards the centre.

By contrast, Luke's Gospel tells, from the very outset, of a different power —of the sure and purposeful movement of the Holy Spirit. And Bethlehem reveals this power of promise, of God's grace reaching through time as surely as Roman rule reached across the earth. For God shapes the future from the past, yet often in ways that surprise, transcend and bypass our human expectations and structures.

Our great cities today speak of secular power, of institution and government, of wealth and grandeur, control and organization. Such power is not all bad, thank God. It can do much good, but it can sometimes be harsh and insensitive, and even at its best, there are areas of human welfare it cannot reach. The Church of Jesus Christ represents a different sort of power. Even in the city, amid the anonymity, beneath the shadow of government and big business, we speak and act for the kingdom of Bethlehem, for the gentle strength of humility, service and love. And this power carries the momentum and mission of the Spirit of God.

For prayer

Pray for anyone you know who exercises public authority and responsibility, that they will be wise, fair and careful in all their work.

Final destination

The middle part of Luke's Gospel portrays Jesus' ministry as a great journey (see, for example, 9:51; 13:22) from Galilee in northern Palestine to Israel's capital Jerusalem. This short reading looks ahead to the end of the journey. No one knows whether all the material in these five verses was spoken on one occasion, or whether the two halves of the passage (31–33 and 34–35) were brought together later, when the sayings of Jesus were collected. But the passage as it now stands highlights some major issues about leadership and care.

Fox and chickens

Herod Antipas was ruler of Galilee. He had executed Jesus' forerunner, John the Baptist, and was evidently gunning for Jesus too. Jesus calls Herod a fox (v. 32). History shows Herod as a foxy character indeed—a devious operator, a political survivor, always concerned and careful to guard his own interests. Jesus means to keep one step ahead of him: foxes are not to be trusted.

The chickens (v. 34) are the people of Jerusalem. Jesus talks of offering them shelter, like a hen gathering her brood under her wing and drawing them into cover in time of danger. The gentle love of God, like shadowing wings, holds all harm at bay (see Psalm 91:4 and Isaiah 31:5 for similar images in the Old Testament).

But you should never leave a fox in charge of a chicken run. In fact Herod's realm did not include Jerusalem, but the contrast is clear enough. Jesus has spoken of God's protective and healing love, whereas Herod is portrayed as a selfish and destructive leader, concerned with killing rather than healing.

Destiny and desolation

Jerusalem is the place where Jesus must die (v. 33). His journeying is not just a process of avoiding trouble, but has a directed purpose, a sense of progress and an end-point. Jerusalem is his destination and his place of destiny. Often in the Old Testament period, there were direct and dramatic clashes in Jerusalem between Israel's prophets and the nation's rulers. God's word spoke sharply to the political powers, and when the criticism stung and the leaders smarted, the consequences for the prophet could be severe. Some had been martyred, yet even their dying brought a word from God, a challenge to the nation's leadership and life. A prophet's message is best spoken at the place of power. It would not do for a prophet to perish away from Jerusalem (v. 33).

For Jerusalem, too, the clash with Jesus will be costly. He talks of her as a deserted city, a desolate house which will not see him truly until she sees him as king (v. 35). He may be echoing the prophet Jeremiah (22:5): a city badly led will become an empty city. Again the issue is leadership. Jesus was warmly appreciated by many of his fellow Jews; it was chiefly the nation's rulers who opposed him. In any society, the people with influence and control often find issues of justice and renewal hard to face; for them prophets are suspect rather than welcome.

Centre and care

So Jesus comes to Jerusalem, to 'Mother Zion' (Isaiah 66:10–11), and offers her children a care that their leaders have not given. He challenges the foxes of his world and deals in healing, help and wholeness (v. 32). Yet he finds himself drawn to pain and passion. Speaking God's word in a city whose power-brokers will not hear, his own script leads him on to suffer.

Many a city claims to love its people. But that love cannot always be delivered when leaders cling too tightly to their position. As in the time of Jesus, there is often work to be done by people of faith and love, work that official structures may overlook—care to give, hurt to resolve, wounds to heal, lives to mend. Still there remains a role for the prophet, for the person who speaks out, whose insight and values can challenge and counter the formal and the accepted. And the role of the prophet carries no guarantee of comfort or ease. The completion of the work (v. 32) may involve the witness of weakness and pain.

For reflection

Where do you see gaps in the caring structures of your city,
that you or your church could do something to fill?

Tears of a king

Jesus was an emotional person. He was moved by his experiences and by other people's responses to him and to God. But rarely do we see him in tears—only at the grave of a dear friend (John 11:35), and here, as he contemplates the death of a beloved city.

Mixed moods

This reading sets joy and grief side by side—excitement and dismay, triumph and tragedy, pain and praise. Through these contrasts we see the hopes and the hurts that surround the name of Jerusalem. On one hand she is the 'city of the great king' (Psalm 48:2), the touching place between heaven and earth. Here the royal presence of Israel's God is known. And Jesus is herald of God's kingdom, the young Prince who comes to kindle Israel's faith and to proclaim the loving rule of her God. No wonder that pilgrims welcome him as he rides by. Here is a king to quicken memories and hopes in Israel (v. 38).

Yet Jesus himself cannot enter into the festival mood of his followers. As he gazes at the city from the Mount of Olives he is overtaken by tears. He suddenly glimpses a dreadful mismatch between what Jerusalem was meant to be and what she will become.

View of war

About 40 years after Jesus' time, there was a major Jewish revolt against the occupying Roman power. For a while the rebels succeeded, but in time the Roman armies returned, besieged Jerusalem, and eventually captured and destroyed it in AD70. Luke's Gospel may have been written shortly after AD70, with memories of these events painfully in mind. Yet the wording of verses 43–44 is not a precise record of the siege of Jerusalem. It echoes some Old Testament passages about war. It looks as if Jesus himself foresaw the fall of the city, and spoke of it in scriptural terms.

Jesus was a shrewd observer of the public mood of his day. He knew that the pressures of Roman rule, and the anger and pride of many Jews, would lead his people eventually to revolt, and on to defeat and disaster. The city did not recognize 'the things that make for peace' (v. 42). Nor did she understand her 'visitation from God' (v. 44), the moment of opportunity that Jesus' coming gave her.

Eyes for peace

So what would 'make for peace'? A more positive response to Jesus' kingdom message is what the passage suggests. Though many acclaimed his entry to the city, he encountered a stiff core of opposition among some religious leaders (v. 39). It seems that he expected this. For Jesus' distinctive view of God's rule—healings and open relationships, his ready talk of forgiveness, his ability to cross social boundaries and acquaint people in fresh and lively ways with God's love—found a very cautious hearing among Jerusalem's establishment. And Jesus feared for his people: unless they could find a new ease in their relationship with God and neighbour, the course of their national fortunes would surely be turbulent and tragic.

Blind spot

What 'makes for peace' can be hard to see in a big city today. The caution of Jerusalem's leaders is easy to copy when we face the challenge of God's kingdom. Revolt may not beckon but, at least in our individual lives, retreat will. It is easier to stay within circles of safe company rather than invest time and care in the wider peace of the whole community. Working life is often seen in terms of making a living, without asking how (or whether) our work really contributes to the welfare of our neighbour. Decisions about where to live, where to shop, how to vote, and even where to worship, seem private choices, depending only on personal preference and benefit.

Yet Jesus offers a different perspective. In his own troubled land, in a society heavy with pressures and complications, he pointed his people to the promise of God's kingdom. His words—and his tears—invite Christians today to look beyond the pressure points that beset our living, and to discover afresh what will 'make for peace' in our cities.

Prayer

Lord Jesus, teach us to us weep with you for the city's brokenness and blindness, and to work with you for its wholeness and healing.

From Jerusalem
to the world

City for the world

Our last two readings suggested a gloomy view of Jerusalem, as the place where Jesus met his most stubborn and decisive opposition. That is far from the whole truth, however. Jerusalem was also the city of resurrection, ascension and Pentecost, the launching point for the worldwide Christian mission. From Jerusalem the word of the Lord goes out (Isaiah 2:3), under the impulse of God's Holy Spirit.

Back to the Bible

The story of Pentecost is full of resonances with the Old Testament. The rush of a mighty wind (v. 2) recalls God's first creative breath on the formless waters (Genesis 1:2). That same creative power is stirring again to renew the face of the earth.

Tongues of fire (v. 3) remind readers of the Exodus story. Pentecost was an occasion when Jews commemorated the giving of their ancient law, when God descended in fire on Mount Sinai (Exodus 19:18). Now fire comes again, sign of the liberating God of Exodus, releasing his people to take good news to the world.

The strange communication (vv. 6–8) is like an undoing of Babel (Genesis 11; see pages 10–11). Jewish pilgrims from far afield had gathered for the Pentecost festival. Their lands of origin (vv. 9–11) stretched from Italy to Iran, about 1000 miles in each direction. But in contrast to Babel, where tongues were scattered and confused, here are voices that cross the boundaries of human language. The Spirit creates understanding, connects people where they have been divided, and communicates the reality of God in ways that transcend human limits. In reaching up to God at Babel, human effort dissolved into incoherence. When God's Spirit comes down at Pentecost, hearts and minds are drawn together.

Out to the nations

Some Jewish writing from this era describes Jerusalem as the navel of the earth, the place from which the whole world draws its life. (There is a trace of this idea in Ezekiel 38:12.) Here at Pentecost Jerusalem becomes in a fresh way a source of life for the nations. The gathering of pilgrims creates an opportunity for the gospel of Jesus to spread abroad. People will hear, many of them will believe (v. 41), and they will carry the message back home. These pilgrims are both Jewish and international—Jewish by race, international by place. Their presence hints strongly that the Christian message, though rooted strongly in Judaism, will cross many cultural and geographical boundaries in reaching the wider world.

One writer points out[10] that the movement is centrifugal rather than centripetal. The nations are not sucked in to Jerusalem, as if by a magnet or whirlpool, but all through the book of Acts the word moves outwards (1:8), like the scattering of seed in a swirling wind.

Paradox and potential

The New Testament offers no simple verdict on Jerusalem. It is a city both of opposition and of opportunity. Its story mirrors the complexity of our human nature, the ways that we mix response and resistance in our dealing with God. Yet in Jerusalem we see the persistence of God's purpose and love: the events that led to the crucifixion did not rub out God's intention. He still used this place to reach the world.

Still God knows the possibilities and the pains of city life. Every big community is a mixture of pain and potential. Urban living reveals some of the hardest edges and ugliest features of our humanity. Yet cities are often places where peoples and nations come close together, and very different cultures find their way into contact and communication. From cities ideas and ideologies go out, fashions and faith can spread, and new groups may hear and discover the gospel.

We cannot re-enact Pentecost—it was a unique moment, as Jerusalem is a unique place—but we can pray for deeper openness to God's Spirit and for fresh opportunities to spread the faith. And we may find, in the multicultural tapestry that is our city life, threads that will lead the message of Christ into new places and among new peoples.

For prayer

Pray for a deeper openness to the work of the Spirit—not for your own sake, but for service to others.

Where three worlds meet

Our last reading was a snapshot of one moment in Jerusalem. But many other cities in the ancient world were international in make-up, as are many cities today. The languages spoken on the pavements and buses are richly varied; the pattern of faces in the streets is multi-coloured. Tourism, politics, business and migration have shrunk the planet, drawn us together and mingled us in mixed and cosmopolitan communities. This mingling has enormous potential for the strength and spread of the Christian faith.

In the first century AD, Syrian Antioch was one of the biggest cities in the Mediterranean world. With a population in hundreds of thousands, it was the main administrative centre for the Roman province of Syria. At Antioch three worlds came together—Jewish, Greek and Roman. There was a large Jewish community, for the Jews were even then a widely scattered people. The main local language was Greek, for the Greek king Alexander had conquered Syria 400 years earlier, and had stamped the place with his own country's speech and culture. Finally, Antioch was a Roman city, holding together provincial life with a shifting company of soldiers, civil servants and business people serving duty there.

Contact for Christ

A few years after Pentecost the church in Jerusalem ran into serious tensions and opposition. Many Christians, including it seems the most open in outlook, left town to settle elsewhere. As they travelled they spoke about their faith. In Antioch these conversations stretched across a major social barrier: Jewish Christians made Gentile converts (vv. 20–21). Suddenly the Christian faith was no longer a sub-species of Judaism. It had started to become a word for the world.

It was almost bound to be Antioch. This was a city where Jewish and Gentile people already mixed; where contact, at least in some circles, was open and friendly; where relationships could span the ethnic barrier. Where friendship can be shared, faith can too. So it was in Antioch that a strong Gentile church first came into being and Jewish and Greek Christians treated one another as brothers and sisters, eating and worshipping together. The pastoral graces of Barnabas and the teaching gifts of Saul gave these Christians a growing love for Christ and for each other (vv. 23-26). Their neighbours noticed.

In a name

In Antioch 'the disciples were first called "Christians"' (v. 26). This new name reflects the three worlds of Antioch. The idea is Jewish, coming from deep in the Old Testament. A 'Messiah'—meaning 'anointed one'—would be marked out by God to represent and bring about his purpose in the world. The word 'Christ' is Greek, translating the Hebrew word 'Messiah'. Finally the ending '-ians' comes from Latin, the Roman language of government. This ending was often used to label the followers of a political or civic figure, as a distinctive group in society, clustered around their leader.

The word 'Christians' may have been coined by Romans in Antioch, to describe people who followed a leader they called 'Christ'. They had become a separate group, visibly distinct from their neighbours. Because their fellowship in Jesus spanned an ethnic divide, others had noticed it.

Out of Antioch

The outreach of this church in Antioch still goes on. Their message is that a multi-ethnic church can attract attention more strongly than a monochrome fellowship. People ask what brings us together across the divide. A varied company of Christians is a witness to its leader, who still gives his people a distinctive identity of their own.

A multi-ethnic city is a setting where the gospel may speak with unusual power. It was surely no coincidence that the church at Antioch quickly got involved in famine relief (vv. 27–30) and in sponsoring wider mission work (13:1–3). This was a community already accustomed to crossing boundaries, to looking beyond immediate horizons, to following new possibilities with God.

Give thanks for mixed and multi-ethnic cities, where Christian faith can bridge and bind different peoples, and the church can see with expanding vision the wide purpose of God.

Prayer

Widen our vision, Lord, to see and love our neighbours, near and far.

Rough reception

Our readings now trace the mission of the Church as it moves out of the lands of the eastern Mediterranean to reach the cities of Greece. Paul and his companions adopted a deliberate strategy in their travels. They concentrated on major centres of population, aiming to establish a bridgehead for the gospel in the cities, from where it could spread through the surrounding areas.

Looking up

Thessalonica was a seaport and administrative centre, with a population in the tens of thousands. A prosperous and privileged place, it was careful to cultivate its good relationship with Rome. A temple had been built to the Roman emperor, and major sporting events were staged in his honour. But official religion of this kind was little more than a veneer on the city's political ambition.

There was a Jewish community in Thessalonica too, and Paul and his friends visited the synagogue, to speak of Jesus as Israel's Messiah. There was a mixed reception here: some Jews believed, as did many of the 'devout Greeks' (v. 4). Many thoughtful Greeks in this period had taken an interest in Judaism. They were attracted by the Jews' commitment to one God and by their emphasis on godly behaviour. Some of these 'devout Greeks'—seekers and enquirers already—proved very receptive to the Christian gospel in these early years (for an example, see Acts 13:43).

Wrong way up

Before long some vigorous opposition arose, stirred up by members of the synagogue and drawing in both the lawless of the city (v. 5) and its lawkeepers (vv. 6–9). The motive may have been religious, but the charges were political: 'turning the world upside-down' (v. 6), breaking imperial laws, and speaking of a strange and subversive kingdom (v. 7).

The only way to quell the trouble and protect the missionaries was for them to leave town, surreptitiously and swiftly (v. 10). After that, almost all we hear about this new church comes from the two Thessalonian letters.

1 Thessalonians in particular tells of the warm response the gospel evoked (1:5–6), of the commitment made by Gentiles to the Christian faith (1:9), of opposition and persecution (2:2, 14), and of the missionaries' pastoral concern for their new converts (2:5–12). When some local Christians died—possibly as a result of the persecution—there was great sorrow and uncertainty about what would become of them (4:13). This church, which had come into being so hurriedly, still had much to learn about its faith.

Mixed messages

There can be many responses in a community to a new idea or movement, as there were when the gospel came to Thessalonica.

- Public values and a concern for stability will easily be offended by anything that seems to divide and disturb. Commitment to the rule of Christ sometimes does challenge convention, habit or ideology. We do serve a different kingdom, an upside-down order of things, that inverts many of the values and standards around us. We cannot (nor should we) always conceal that.
- If religion figures in a shallow way in many people's lives, some will start to look for a deeper reality. They may find their way into churches, looking for integrity of faith and character in those they meet there.
- Trouble can arise if one religious group is seen to violate the integrity or space of another. That is a vexed issue for churches in multi-faith communities, concerned for good relationships but with a gospel to advocate too. The right approach locally is usually best worked out by local people.
- Pastoral nurture matters for new Christians. Whoever said, 'Sincerity is the key; if you can fake that, you'll be all right,' was not describing true Christian care. Something more than fake sincerity—a deep, active and costly concern for the people we serve—is the only way to help Christians grow. Paul and his companions worked for their living rather than asking for support from their converts (1 Thessalonians 2:9).

Someone kept the two Thessalonian letters. This church must have survived, despite the stresses and sorrows of their early days in the faith. What God starts, he can sustain better than we might expect.

For reflection

Are there varied attitudes in your local community to the witness of the church?
Is that a problem or an opportunity?

Anything new

Athens was a city whose days of power had passed. No longer the principal political centre in Greece (as she has become again today), she was a comparatively small place, sidelined by the Roman colonial power. Yet Athens was still the centre of Greek educational life. There were strong and active intellectual traditions, stretching back through the centuries. Groups of philosophers met in the great market square and revelled in new ideas to debate (vv. 17–22).

Mind matters

Athens in the New Testament stands for the city as a centre of learning, a place where ideas are formed and theories and opinions discussed. Here Christianity speaks to the world of thought. And Paul's message to the men of Athens is like no other Christian preaching in the New Testament. Elsewhere we hear addresses to Jewish audiences, or in one case to a more rural Gentile audience. But this is the only New Testament preaching addressed to sophisticated, urban Gentiles. Paul's starting point, and his line of approach, are chosen with his audience in mind. For these people know much, yet they understand very little about the gospel or its background in Judaism.

Knowing and unknowing

Paul's speech has three main themes:
- **God is known:** Paul comments on how strangely superstitious Athens appears to be. There is even an altar 'to an unknown God' (v. 23)—like an insurance policy, in case their collection of statues and temples had left any gods out. It is rather like the fear of walking under a ladder or of living at number thirteen. Against that background—of life lived in a fog of ignorance and uncertainty, despite all of this city's learning—Paul sets out to tell of the God he knows (v. 23).
- **God is near:** One school of Greek philosophy, the Epicureans (v. 18), thought of the gods as being remote and detached. The Epicurean ideal

was a calm, ordered life, undisturbed and unruffled, somewhat with-drawn from mundane stresses. But life is not like that: it is a network of bonds and belonging, and these are often costly and awkward. And God too is deeply involved, committed to the world he has made (vv. 24–28), the author and hub of all our relationships.

- **God notices:** God is not cornered by human worship. He is independent (vv. 24, 25, 29). Perhaps this thought was addressed especially to the Stoic philosophers. Their big idea was 'self-sufficiency'—being strong enough to cope with life on our own. But we are not self-sufficient. God is, and we depend on him. God overlooks our ignorance (v. 30), the faults and follies that come because we do not know any better, but he expects us to take seriously what he has shown us of right and wrong.

Finally, these three themes converge in the message of the risen Jesus (v. 31), our companion, the sign of God's presence among us, and the world's judge.

Present Christ

Paul took seriously the issues that mattered to his audience. He talked their language and tackled their concerns. Every age needs Christian thinkers who will do as Paul did, who will engage with the sharp minds and deep questions of their day, and offer honest and wise responses. And as we press towards understanding, over and again we shall find how deeply the wisdom of God is made known in Jesus. His life, his example, his suffering and his resurrection help us to make sense of human experience in God's world.

A society that can think deeply may still be fog-bound when it comes to knowing God. The Church tells of God who is known on earth, who is committed to a costly, loving relationship with us, and who is greater than all our self-sufficiency. We tell of manger, cross and empty tomb, and if we tell it truly and honestly, the outcome may be as in Athens (vv. 32–34): some mocked; some wanted to hear more; and some believed.

For reflection

'When the ultimate explanation of things is found in the creating, sustaining, judging and redeeming work of a personal God, then science can be the servant of humanity, not its master.' [11]

Bad for business

A city can be a complex mesh of different interests, group loyalties, concerns and fears. Relationships and commitments interlock. Disturb the system at one point, and movement will surely be felt somewhere else. In Ephesus this complexity led to a near-riot; even an ill-informed crowd can be angry and volatile. The shrewd words of the town clerk managed to defuse the trouble, but once again Paul had to leave town in haste (20:1).

Temple and tourism

Ephesus was the chief city of the Roman province of Asia—the western end of what we call Turkey. With a population of 200,000, the city was a centre for communication and commerce, for court business and for civil administration. Paul spent about two years there (v. 10), drew much attention to the gospel, and challenged the magical traditions and interests that had lured and attracted many people in Ephesus (vv. 18–20).

The pride of Ephesus was the Greek goddess Artemis. Her temple was nearby, and the city felt it had a special relationship with her. The people gave her their worship and reverence, and she blessed them with protection and prosperity. Although there were other temples to Artemis around Asia and the Mediterranean, Ephesus was regarded as the headquarters, the heart of Artemis worship. Anyone who challenged Artemis was seen to be insulting and demeaning Ephesus.

The incident described in our reading probably took place in the spring. Paul had just sent two colleagues ahead of him to Greece (v. 22), and this suggests that the summer travelling season was beginning. 'About that time' (v. 23) of the year, two major festivals were held in Ephesus. These brought interested visitors to town, who would spend money and take home souvenirs and objects of devotion. Silver models of the Artemis temple sold well (v. 24), and there would be some resentment of any activity or movement that distracted people's attention from the big occasion.

Artisans for Artemis

The silversmiths were the first to speak of a threat to Artemis. They were sensitive to their sales figures, and must have noticed—or feared—a drop in business as the Christian message made its impact. Well-organized trade guilds were a feature of this era, and these men acted together to arouse public indignation, and to cast the issue as a threat to the good of the city.

The theatre (v. 29) was an outdoor venue, holding about 20,000, and a natural meeting place for any major civic event. But there was no great meeting of minds on this occasion (v. 32). When Alexander the Jew tried to speak, perhaps to distance the city's Jewish community from Paul's activity, he made no headway at all. Loud voices and strong feelings drowned him out (v. 34). Eventually the town clerk quietened everybody. The empire would act severely against disorderly cities (v. 40), and he was anxious to contain the situation. By the end it seems that the Christians are to be left alone, unless court charges can be brought.

Speed and sensitivity

Things can happen quickly in a city. Rumours can spread, growing as they go, with something of a snowball quality about them. They can melt like snow too, and vanish as if they had never been.

Paul's preaching touched a tender spot. Ephesus cared very much about Artemis, and believed that she cared for Ephesus. An early statement of Christian belief was 'Jesus is Lord' (1 Corinthians 12:3). But you cannot say, 'Jesus is Lord' without challenging the supremacy of other gods and lords. There is a controversial edge to Christian faith, the so-called 'scandal of particularity'.[12]

'The gospel is always at its most controversial when it comes into conflict with economic interests.'[13] Money talks, and money gets very edgy if its supply lines are threatened. Any Christian challenge to vested economic interests is likely to provoke strong anger. But some ways of money-making are highly questionable. Jesus warned his friends to beware when all speak well of us (Luke 6:26). If we are determined never to make any enemies, perhaps we shall never do much good either.

Prayer

Lord, give your Church wisdom and courage, not to seek controversy,
and not to hide Christ.

Dual citizenship

Twin city

Philippi in northern Greece was a town with a past. It was recognized as a 'colony', a little copy of Rome, a distant outpost of the empire's capital. Colony status was an honour. There were privileges and tax breaks. Many people in Philippi held Roman citizenship, and were proud of the link. They were members of two communities at once.

But the Christian church in Philippi would be a mixed company. Not all would count as citizens. Many would be poor. Some would be slaves. So Paul writes to tell them, not of high worldly privilege, but of a very different link. 'Our citizenship is in heaven' (3:20). These Christians belonged to the community of the risen Christ, of which their local church was just a branch. But it was an outpost whose citizens held all the privileges and responsibilities of the centre. The church in Philippi was an out-station of the kingdom of heaven, and its members were to live by the patterns and customs of that kingdom.

Living the gospel

The idea of belonging surfaces early in the letter: 'Live your life in a manner worthy of the gospel of Christ' (1:27). The phrase 'live your life' means more precisely 'exercise your citizenship', live as a member of a community. Christians should conduct their daily lives in a way that matches the good news they believe. Paul spells out what this will mean.

- **Cost:** The church in Philippi was born amid persecution and opposition (Acts 16:11–40). These people had encountered hostility for their faith. Our reading underlines that experience: 'Standing... striving... suffering... struggling' (1:27, 29, 30). This church might still expect to get hurt. They were a minority; they were breaking ranks by abandoning their loyalty to the old gods of Greece and Rome. Their new faith was not a comfortable Christianity, but a demanding and testing commitment.

- **Care**: Standing up to pressure depends on holding together. Unity matters: 'One spirit… one mind' (1:27). This letter aims to unite its readers, and reminds them of the need to support one another and stick together. Unity is a practical business, working itself out in life's ordinary encounters and relationships. So the opening verses of chapter 2 speak of everyday virtues —kindness, mutual support, humility, unselfishness, and making an effort to agree (vv. 1–4). A group of people who can live like this will be able to handle pressure creatively; those who cannot may get driven apart.
- **Christ**: The source, the template, where these Christian virtues start, is Jesus. 'Let the same mind be in you that was in Christ Jesus' (2:5). What Christians can be for one another comes from our bond with him. True mutual commitment comes from the Servant King. The 'Christ-hymn' of 2:6–11 tells of Jesus giving himself, pouring himself into our human life, and showing us the true nature of God by the ways he served and suffered. For this, God honoured him and raised him high.
- **Commitment**: Finally we come right back down from heaven to earth. 'So then, dear friends, act out the reality of your salvation' (2:12). Jesus is the template. His way of humble service is God's pattern for the Church, and is strong enough to sustain unity, even when pressure and opposition come. This is how Christians are to 'live worthy of the gospel of Christ', acting out from day to day the Church's link with the kingdom of heaven.

Double belonging

Christians are still citizens of two realms—earth and heaven. We belong to our local communities and serve the places where we are set. (Our reading in Jeremiah 29, pages 42–43, expresses this very clearly.) We live as citizens of heaven, too, following the pattern of life we find in Jesus Christ. That commitment can unite us as Christians and give us courage and confidence in tough times. And it will have a strength and savour of its own to sustain and season every community we join and every company we keep.

So city Christians have a double loyalty—commitment to the city, and commitment to the way of Christ. For only by following Christ can we truly love the people among whom we live.

Prayer

Lord Jesus Christ, when we come under pressure, help us to seek and follow your way, that our lives may be worthy of your good news.

Foolishness of God

We know more about Corinth than any other New Testament church, from Paul's two letters to the Christians there. This church was full of problems, and most of these arose from the sort of city Corinth was—a town on the make, where wealthy and powerful people were very conscious of their status. We can track four features in Corinth's background that shaped the city and its church.

Contours of a culture

- **Patronage**: Corinth was a Roman colony, part of a great pyramid of rank and privilege that ran from the Emperor down through provincial governors and local dignitaries. It was an aggressive, competitive place. Wealthy people were appointed to public office, office conferred power, and power gave opportunities for making money. Lower down the social scale, too, there were hierarchies and clusters of loyalty and support. Contacts mattered. Social climbing was a major industry.
- **Politics**: The Greek cities had a long-standing heritage of political energy and rivalry. Factions would form around popular leaders. Men were eager to seek position or prestige, whether in public office or in smaller groups, such as business guilds or religious associations.
- **Philosophy**: The intellectual tradition of the Greek world placed a high value on wisdom, education and eloquence. Showy, polished speaking was a strong social asset.
- **Priesthood**: There is some evidence that upper-class people tended to take the lead in religious affairs and ceremonies.

Culture and church

We read that 'not many' (v. 26) of the Corinthian Christians were educated, powerful or from wealthy families. This is hardly surprising, for most people in Corinth were poor. But some better-off members of the church were causing difficulties out of all proportion to their numbers. They imported into church life (perhaps without realizing it) the habits and instincts of the secular world.

Paul writes of quarrels, factions and rivalries (3:1–5), of a church divided at the Lord's Supper (11:18), and of the need for Christians to honour one another (12:14–26). The élitism and snobbery, the hunger for prominence, the pride and pomposity that shaped public life in Corinth were affecting church life too.

A different wisdom

Paul writes very directly about the cross of Jesus right at the start of this letter. This is the baseline for all his advice to this church. The humility of Christ contrasts sharply with Corinthian pride. But the cross is not a foolish thing. It is rather the sign of a different wisdom, of a God who challenges human arrogance and bypasses the world's orders of rank and position. If the Corinthian Christians can understand the cross, then they will grow into a healthy church. They will start to learn a different kind of lifestyle, marked not by arrogance and competition, but by humility and concern for the common good.

Culture and gospel

Who takes the lead in the Christian Church today? As in Corinth, it can often be the people who are leaders in other spheres of life, for they have gifts that others admire and follow. Their practised leadership can be of great worth. But the habits we learn in the secular world will not always serve the church well, nor always reflect the values of the gospel.

This letter urges that we place our first emphasis on the cross of Christ—not just as a gift to trust but as a pattern to follow, too. In modern secular society, as in ancient Corinth, resources often mean power. Money, management skills and knowledge can give control over other people's lives. But a church shaped by the cross will have a very different atmosphere. Christ's sacrifice makes a radical difference.

If we take him seriously, we may not act selfishly; we cannot honour him by despising or dominating our sisters and brothers; we need not strive to attract attention if we truly understand what he has done for us. Even the gifts the world values—finance, organization and wise speech—we may offer in the church humbly, for the sake of others. We give of our substance and ourselves —not for control, but as contributions to the whole life of the body of Christ.

For prayer

Pray that the values of Christ may be contagious, and may seep into the life of the wider community through the life of your church.

Philemon

Turning point

This shortest of Paul's letters was written from prison, probably from Ephesus or Rome. Philemon was a well-to-do Christian who lived at Colossae, some distance away. The letter concerns Onesimus, a slave in Philemon's household.

So far as we can piece the story together, it goes something like this. Onesimus fell out with his master—we do not know why—and ran off. Like many a fugitive, he went to the big city. Once there, someone urged him to seek out Paul, who was being held under house arrest. Paul was a friend of his master and might be able to do something to restore the situation.

At some stage Onesimus came to Christian faith—possibly through Paul's influence, if that is what Paul means by 'whose father I have become' (v. 10). So Paul now writes to Philemon to ask that Onesimus be received back, 'no longer as a slave, but more than a slave, a beloved brother' (v. 16).

Far from home

The big city is often a refuge for the person whose home situation has gone irretrievably and irreconcilably wrong. Here is a place to merge into the crowd, to lose the past and try some new possibilities. Of course, it may not work out: decent accommodation, steady work and real friends are not always easily come by, and good decisions are harder to take on unfamiliar turf. The city may offer promise but it claims its casualties too.

So Onesimus is a patron saint for the runaway, the new arrival on the long-distance bus, the eyes scanning the shop ads, the face at the window of the squat. He comes out of an unhappy relationship, he travels to an unfamiliar place and hopes to sort things out. And eventually he goes back. For him, the city proves to be a turning point rather than a staging post or a stopping place. But he goes back as a different person, with a Christian faith he can call his own. And, if Paul's advice is taken, Onesimus will go back to a changed relationship, to a household reshaped by the gospel.

Cause for challenge

Today slavery is totally unacceptable, and we may question why Paul sends Onesimus back to it. Why did the early Christians not protest against the whole business? The answer is probably bound up with the size of the Christian movement at this stage. They had not the clout to challenge major social institutions head-on. None the less, this letter, calling the slave a brother, strikes me as a slow-burning fuse, undermining the whole spirit of slavery. It is a cause for shame that some nations with a long Christian tradition were so slow to act on this, but it is a point for credit that among the most persistent abolitionist voices were those of committed Christian people.

Resources for reconciliation

'More than a slave, a beloved brother' (v. 16). Paul sends Onesimus to a home that will have to adjust to his coming. The issue of status in the house, of rank, duty and ownership, will not count in the way it did before. The naming of a fellow Christian as 'brother' or 'sister' sets us, at the deepest level of relationship, on even ground. We are one body in Christ, committed to one another's good; we notice, care, support, encourage.

Paul works hard to persuade Philemon. He speaks of a family affair, of Christians as 'brother', 'sister' and 'father' (vv. 1, 2, 7, 10, 16, 20). He writes of the faith and love at the heart of all our common life (vv. 5–6). He acknowledges the difficulties involved (vv. 11, 15, 18): a spirit of forgiveness will be needed. Facing each other as brothers will involve overcoming a sense of hurt and wrong, for both men.

Certainly Paul applies moral pressure. He led Philemon to faith; this is pay-back time (vv. 19–21). Philemon would surely feel some constraint. But the letter survived, which suggests he took it seriously. And some decades later we hear of a Christian bishop in Ephesus called Onesimus. Was this the same person, now released from slavery? Perhaps the city was indeed a turning point, a stepping-stone to freedom in more ways than one.

For reflection

How readily do you treat fellow Christians as sister and brother?
Is this harder or easier if the other person has a different background from yours?
And what happens to our sense of being one family in Christ when we have a serious disagreement?

The state we live in

The ancient city of Rome was the control centre of a wide empire. Here decisions were taken, provincial governors and small-time kings appointed, armies ordered to and fro, laws written and taxes gathered in. Not that all was wisely or honestly done. When this letter was sent, in about AD56, the notorious emperor Nero had just come to the throne. The initial hopes held out for his reign, after the megalomaniac Caligula and the somewhat eccentric Claudius, eventually foundered badly. By the time Nero died in 68, public affairs were in a sorry mess.

The Christian church in Rome lived in the shadow of big government, and surely without any illusions that the authorities always get things right. Yet Paul is remarkably positive about the role of the state, and offers a very solid base for a Christian view of government. There is nothing like this in Paul's other writing. So why does this material come at this place, in this letter? There may be two reasons, and both reflect the current situation in Rome.

Payments and persecution

- **Tolls and taxes**: A secular writer from the ancient world tells of unrest in Rome over tax just at this period. Collectors were allowed to take a substantial mark-up for themselves, and there were serious public protests about the overall tax burden on the people. It seems that Paul has heard of this trouble brewing, and warns the Christians not to get caught up. They were a vulnerable group, and Paul may have been anxious to prevent them getting into needless quarrels. So the last verse of this short section on the state (v. 7) tells the readers very directly to pay their various taxes and dues; this may be the advice to which the whole paragraph has been leading.

- **Trials and troubles**: The second factor is justice. Paul has been writing about revenge: even when other people disturb and distress you, do not hit back. Leave the matter for God to deal with, and respond to evil with active goodness (12:17–21). The section about the state follows this teaching and meshes with it. While we wait for the final judgment of God (12:19), our civil authorities exist to restrain evil, to keep the peace and to protect the life of the community (13:3). The Christian should support that work, by contributing to it (13:6–7) and by proper submission to its authority (13:1–5).

So both the public outcry over taxation and the Christians' private tribulations give Paul cause to write about government—why it is there, what it ought to do and the attitude Christians should take to it.

There for a reason

Government has a purpose under God: to deter and punish evil, and to promote good (13:3–4). Government is a gift from God. Of course, our rulers are not perfect, but the general effect of having some government rather than none will be the protection of goodness and the restraint of wrongdoing. So we submit to rulers as part of our service to God and neighbour. We pray for them too (1 Timothy 2:1–2), because their work is difficult and important.

But if a government fails to deliver, it may be a Christian duty to remind rulers of their responsibilities. There is a long tradition of frank criticism among the Old Testament prophets. And if a perverse state authority does the very opposite of what it ought—if it practises and promotes blatant injustice—some Christians question whether it may claim our loyalty and submission at all: Romans 13 may cease to apply.

Debts and duties

Public authorities, national and local, continue to play a major part in our living. They collect our taxes, take responsibility for important services and draft the laws under which we live. We owe them, so far as we can conscientiously give, our submission and support. But first we owe them our prayers. For if we pray, our support will be discerning, and our criticism constructive.

Beyond all this we owe our neighbour the constant debt of love (13:8). However worthy or unsatisfactory our earthly authorities turn out to be, the Church lives by the beacon of hope that is the new dawn of God's coming kingdom (13:11–13).

For thought and prayer

Does 'submitting' to authority mean just putting up with it?
If not, what is the difference in your area at the moment?

Welcome one another

Separate paths and patterns

The press of big city life does not always help churches to work together. When people travel a distance to worship, when there is a wide choice of churches within a couple of miles, when churches have quite different styles, then local congregations can get very caught up in their own life. We forget Christ's other friends, our brothers and sisters in neighbouring parishes and fellowships. And when we do try to work together, differences of tradition and habit sometimes prevent easy co-operation.

The same problems affected Christians in Rome in the first century. Some of them were Jews, and some Gentiles. They had different customs, expectations and contacts. Christians from a Jewish background continued to value traditional ways as set out in the Jewish law. Their calendar was thick with fasts and festivals. There were meats to avoid, and Jews would even avoid oil and wine if there was any suspicion that a portion of the crop had been offered to a Greco-Roman god; for them, that would contaminate the whole consignment. Gentile Christians would not be greatly concerned about these matters. Why should their conduct be determined by other people's prejudices?

It is hardly surprising that a number of Christian groups met separately. Differences over food might raise sharp difficulties when Christians ate together and shared Holy Communion. People found it more convenient to mix with fellow Christians of their own kind, with a similar outlook and background. But this sort of separation is a poor second-best. Throughout his letter to the Romans Paul has explained how Christ died for Jew and Gentile alike, and that neither group has a preferred place in Christ's family. Now he tackles some of the practical issues.

At home with one another

The big word is 'welcome'. This section of the letter begins, 'Welcome one another, but not in order to argue' (v. 1). Even when opinions and practices differ, Christians may look on one another as people whom 'God has welcomed' (v. 3). Then at the climax of this section, drawing together all the practical material, 'Welcome one another, therefore, just as Christ has welcomed you, for the glory of God' (15:7). In between comes the tough but gentle advice about how and why welcome matters. Paul makes two main points.

- **Space for a neighbour:** Christians should realize that there are different views in the Church. Jews do not need to abandon all their Jewishness to come to Christ, nor need Gentiles be dragged into being Jews. In our actions and opinions (vv. 4–6), in our living and our dying (v. 7–9), and as we face God's judgment (vv. 10–12), our first responsibility is to God. We cannot compel a fellow Christian to see things exactly our way.
- **Sensitivity to a neighbour:** All of that sounds like a charter for complete freedom: love God and do what you like. But the second half of this chapter is about sensitivity. Food and drink, for example, is not at the heart of Christianity (v. 17), but if something as mundane as my eating and drinking will wreck another Christian's faith, then I should abstain (v. 21). Liberty of conscience does not always mean liberty of conduct. Restricting and restraining our own behaviour to help someone else hold the faith can be a real act of love—not a harsh duty or compulsion, but a glad gift to the body of Christ.

Crossing the street

When we cross the street to meet Christians of another hue, Paul's advice may follow us: Be helpful. Don't major on points of disagreement (v. 1). When you greet a brother or sister in Christ, aim to bind the Church together, not to spend your time widening its fissures and fault-lines. And be humble—be ready to back down if your convinced and cheerful liberty is obviously unsettling another person's faith in Christ.

This is not easy to handle. If it were, our churches would not have been divided so long. But even in the hectic pace of the city, our churches will receive more from our Lord, and give more to our communities, if we can welcome and work with all of Christ's friends as our friends too.

For reflection

'We must constantly strive to see that Christ's truth and Christ's love… stand supreme over what we humans want and do.' [14]

Cities unseen

Cultures in contact

Many towns and cities are mentioned in the Bible, but there are some surprising omissions. Two major communities that are often overlooked may have left a distinctive mark on the New Testament. In both places Jewish people came into contact with the life and ways of the wider Gentile world.

Sepphoris - city on a hill

As Jesus was growing up, the most important community in Galilee was Sepphoris, four miles north of Nazareth. When the lands of King Herod the Great were divided among his sons in 4BC, Herod Antipas made this his capital. Sepphoris was well situated, with plenty of fertile land around, and good roads in all directions. It was an understandable choice. Even when Antipas switched his capital to Tiberias in about AD20 Sepphoris remained an important business centre.

Antipas built in style. Here for the first time was a Galilean town with a classy Roman look. Construction work went on for decades using workmen from all over Galilee. Quite possibly Joseph came from Nazareth to work in Sepphoris. He may even have taught his sons their skills there. But, curiously, the Gospels never mention Sepphoris. Did the adult Jesus never visit? Why not? Here are two suggestions.

Not only does Jesus apparently avoid Sepphoris, but we never see him in Tiberias either. He may have deliberately given Herod Antipas a wide berth. For Jesus brought a message about a new kingdom coming, and Antipas as ruler would hardly welcome that—he had already killed John the Baptist for turbulent preaching. So Jesus avoided the two royal towns, kept on the move when Antipas became too curious (see on Luke 13, pages 62–63), and went to places where he could speak more freely.

Secondly, Jesus' parables talk about wealth, work and trade, also about unemployment, poverty and begging. He understood the ways that money, and the lack of it, affected his people. Herod's projects in Sepphoris and Tiberias had changed the economy of Galilee. Wealth became more concentrated than before. Now the land had big towns to feed. Market forces started to play a greater role, and some poorer farmers would get squeezed. Did Jesus deliberately take himself to the smaller, more fragile communities? Was some of his teaching about property, sharing and generosity a response to the effect a big wealthy town like Sepphoris was having on the countryside around?

Alexandria - spreading the light

Alexandria in northern Egypt was one of the largest cities in the ancient world. Hundreds of thousands of people were packed close together on a ridge of land facing the sea. There was a massive Jewish community, and surely some were among the pilgrims from Egypt who heard Peter on the day of Pentecost (Acts 2:10). From the New Testament we learn little of Christian mission here, but the traditions of the Egyptian Coptic Church, still many millions strong, are very ancient indeed. I once asked Egyptian visitors to our church in Britain, 'When was your church founded?' 'AD56,' they replied.

At Alexandria Jewish teachings came into contact with the philosophy of the Greek world, and the city touches the New Testament story in two ways. Here, a couple of centuries before Jesus, the Septuagint was made. This Greek translation of the Old Testament was a bridge between Jewish faith and Gentile culture. It helped Jewish communities around the Mediterranean to keep their religious identity in a Greek-speaking environment. And this was how the Christian message spread so swiftly in the earliest years, using the Greek-speaking synagogues as stepping-stones into the Gentile world. Most of the New Testament authors knew and quoted the Septuagint; they grounded the gospel in Judaism, but in language that Gentiles could understand. The Septuagint helped the gospel of a Jewish Messiah to become an international faith.

From Alexandria an enthusiastic Christian preacher called Apollos sailed to Ephesus and on to Corinth (Acts 18:24–28). He did much good, but perhaps he also contributed to the problems in Corinth. Some Corinthians were easily impressed by knowledge and eloquence (1 Corinthians 1:12; see also pages 80–81). If Apollos' approach offered a smooth bridge between the gospel and the educated traditions of the Greek world, then it was a bridge too far: Corinth overlooked the tough challenge of the cross.

For reflection

Cities concentrate power; they also bring ideas and cultures into contact with one another. There are opportunities and dangers in both of these things.

The city to come

The great unseen city in the New Testament is not on the map at all. It is the city Revelation calls the new Jerusalem, the place where the Bible story itself comes to an end (Revelation 21—22). Some Jewish writing of the New Testament era looked forward to the coming city of God on earth, new and true and glorious. But the letter to the Hebrews speaks in a different way, of a city that is in heaven, both ahead and above, beckoning the Church forward into its life, and lighting the way along the journey.

Book of the road

Hebrews is a book of pilgrimage, a travel guide. It was sent to Christians who were facing persecution for their faith, and struggling to sustain their momentum. It speaks of the Christian life as a journey, and uses stories of pilgrims in Old Testament times to inspire and challenge its readers. A long passage early in the letter takes up the Exodus story of Israel's long journey to the Promised Land (3:7—4:11). 'Press on,' it says, 'to enter the resting place God has prepared for you' (4:9–11).

The idea of a city first appears in chapter 11, as Hebrews taps into the story of another Old Testament pilgrim, Abraham. We earlier described Abraham and Sarah as people who left the city behind (see page 12). Indeed, they lived as wanderers (vv. 8–9). But for Hebrews this was a purposeful journeying— not just walking around but travelling home. They were heading for a city more permanent and better prepared than any on earth (11:10, 16). They were the first travellers in a long procession of faith that leads to a solid and secure destination. The hope that can look beyond the horizon, trust in more than it sees and act on that trust is what Hebrews calls 'faith' (11:1, 8, 13).

City of light and shadow

The city is ahead. Yet, just a chapter later, the readers seem to have got there already: 'You have come…' (12:22). For in one way Christians have a fuller contact with the life of heaven than our Old Testament forebears had: our experience of Jesus and of God's new covenant in Jesus gives a direct line to heaven. Jesus is ascended and the destination is more visible and clearer than it ever was before. His people may come into his presence in their prayers and faith (10:19). And the place to which faith leads is a joyous, awesome, majestic place, rich with company and praise.

Yet on earth the road stretches on, with trials yet to be faced. A Christian is in touch with heaven, but still travelling towards it. As it did for Abraham and Sarah, the journey leads out of town into the wilds. At the very end of this letter, Hebrews reminds the first readers that their life of faith will be tough and demanding. They follow a crucified Lord who was put to death outside the walls of Jerusalem (13:12). His followers too will sometimes be sidelined and abused by neighbours. A Christian is always something of a misfit in society; we belong to a different home. The hope of that city ahead may beckon us into hard and hurtful places; if so, it will be a beckoning nearer to Jesus (13:13–14).

Heaven is a city

So the hope of the city ahead is an invitation to *travel*, to press on as a pilgrim people (11:10, 16). It is an invitation to *tremble* with awe and anticipation as we look to God's great heavenly community (12:22). And it may well be an invitation to *trouble*. If a Christian is edged aside in an earthly community, we remember that Jesus too was treated as an outsider; with him (12:2), we look ahead (13:12–14).

We look to the place the Bible describes as a city. Heaven, in its Bible portrait, is not an escape to the quietness of our individual communion with God. It is certainly the place where we shall be most fully and truly ourselves, but it is not a place of solitude. It is a big community, knit and known. It is a secure place where all hurt and fear are past. It is a grand and glorious place where awe and worship will seem natural.

So living in the city now is an anticipation of the life ahead. Well-made buildings, great crowds, a community that lasts—all point towards the greater city 'whose architect and builder is God' (11:10). And we shall be truly at home when we get there. The Jerusalem above 'is our mother' (Galatians 4:26).

Prayer

Living and eternal God, before whom all time is laid out, and in whom all time is drawn together, may we follow in trust your path into the future. Through Jesus Christ our Lord. Amen.

Final revelation

Letters for seven churches

Where people are

'This place feels it has failed as a town. The churches have lost confidence too, and our witness is not strong.'

'Our town sits in the bend of a river, and we are insular people, not very open to outsiders.'

Those are recent comments by two British Christians about their home towns. Places shape people. Cities affect their churches. In many ways, we become what we belong to. If our wider community is deflated or proud, active or tired, at ease or at odds with itself, that touches the mood of the church.

Revelation was written to seven churches in Asia Minor (western Turkey), and it begins with a direct message to each of the seven. It aims to kindle their faith, to re-stock their minds with God's perspective on the world. Each short letter speaks of Christ, and of the readers' own locality.

Glimpses of Christ

Revelation opens with an overpowering vision of Jesus Christ, who appeared to John as he worshipped (1:9–20). Then it weaves the words and images of this first chapter, a little at a time, into the seven letters that follow. Here, for example, are the introductions to three of the letters:

- **Ephesus:** He who walks among the seven golden lampstands (1:12; 2:1).
- **Smyrna:** He who is the first and the last, who was dead and came to life (1:17–18; 2:8).
- **Thyatira:** He who has eyes like a flame of fire and feet like burnished bronze (1:14–15; 2:18).

The glorious Christ who appeared to John is the same one who comes to the seven churches, amid all their troubles and weaknesses, and meets them too in all his glory, strength and love.

Home territory

As well as this anchor to the start of the book, each letter is laden with echoes of the customs and circumstances of the city to which it is sent.

- **Pergamum**, 'where Satan's throne is' (2:13), was a centre for formal worship of the Roman Emperor. There was a long tradition of worship to rulers, and the temples were intimidatingly grand. When Rome took control, emperor-worship could be used as a test of loyalty, backed up by the power of the sword. Any Christian who refused to bow might be in grave danger. Pergamum already had one martyr (2:13). Should more persecution follow, let the Christians there remember that ultimate power does not belong to the Emperor. It is Jesus who holds 'the sharp two-edged sword' (2:12).

- The people at **Sardis** are told, 'Keep awake!' (3:2). This city stood on a steep hill-top, and had once been captured through lack of vigilance. Was it still a careless, casual place, thinking itself immune to outside pressures? But Christ wants an alert church.

  The 'book of life' (3:5) would have been a more welcome thought in Sardis. This city had been a royal archive centre. God, too, numbers, names and values his people.

- **Philadelphia** receives a confident message, full of permanence and solidity: 'You will never go out' (3:12). After a famous earthquake in the area, there had been after-shocks so persistent and severe that many residents moved out into the country. This city had learned not to trust itself. But it can trust Jesus.

'I know...' begins each letter, and the words and images remind these churches that Christ does indeed know the details and difficulties of his people's life. It is natural, it is inevitable, that churches reflect the pressures and peculiarities of our home communities. But Christ understands our trials and our towns, and the church is a conduit between the local community and his love. Like our towns and cities, the gospel too has a distinctive life and character. It offers hope and strength, which we may share in Jesus' name with the places where we live.

For reflection

What do you think Jesus would say to your church?

Letter to Laodicea

The last of the seven letters is probably the best-known. Laodicea was one of a triangle of towns, along with Colossae and Hierapolis, in the Lycus valley inland from Ephesus. It was a prosperous place in material terms, but the life of the church was not prospering as it ought.

Moderate temperature

'Neither cold nor hot' (v. 15) is an odd description. But these three cities were very differently endowed with natural water supplies. Hierapolis had hot medicinal springs, and Colossae had pure, cold water. Laodicea had very little decent drinking water, and piped its supply from some miles away: even then the water was very hard, and had to stand a while for the sediment to settle. So the first message to this church is, 'You are like your water supply. You neither heal nor refresh. In fact you make me feel sick' (v. 16). The reason why comes in the next verse.

Comfort zone

Laodicea was a contented city, comfortably off and well aware of it. Their sheep produced the finest wool for miles around. There was a medical school, and the area was famous for eye ointment. It was a banking centre too. Money, vision and good clothing were local specialities. They were surely not 'poor, blind, and naked' (v. 17). This place liked to handle its own problems. After a severe earthquake in AD60 Laodicea refused any subsidy from the central funds of the Roman Empire. The citizens preferred to pay for the rebuilding themselves and there were some spectacularly large and ostentatious gifts.

This self-sufficiency had affected the church; they were complacent, content and confident, not even needing the support and company of Christ. Who needs help when you come from Laodicea? So this letter challenges them to review their situation, to turn again to Jesus and to receive his wealth and protection. The sharp words carry not only criticism, but care too: 'I reprove and discipline those whom I love' (v. 19). Jesus invites his church to get to know him at a new depth, to take up again a relationship of dependence and devotion, to stop thinking they have everything under control.

Door of opportunity

The image of Jesus knocking (v. 20) has been used by many a preacher to urge people to 'invite Jesus into your life'. Holman Hunt's famous painting, *The Light of the World*, was inspired by this passage: Jesus the light-bearer waits at the door, but there is no handle visible; the handle is inside. What, though, would the picture have meant in Laodicea? Two suggestions might help.

Laodicea was an administrative centre with roads leading in all directions. Its people would be used to the billeting of civil servants and soldiers on the town, without much politeness or payment. Jesus is more respectful, not imposing himself nor presuming on people's goodwill, but making a courteous approach that respects the integrity of the host.

Another background comes from the frontiers of religion and magic. A host of magical texts from the ancient world speak of elaborate rituals for summoning and securing the help of a god. Some of these involved the setting of a table where worshipper and god would share a meal. If this practice was known in Laodicea, there is an obvious contrast: Jesus takes the initiative, simply and directly. He approaches; he does not wait to be summoned by complex ceremony.

Whatever the exact intention of these words, the general meaning is clear: these Christians are invited to leave their self-sufficiency and renew and refresh their relationship with Jesus.

Plenty and more

Some coins from Laodicea show a 'horn of plenty', a great cone brimming with corn and fruit. This city gladly proclaimed the wealth of its resources. The same mood had affected the church there too. It's hard to be committed when you're comfortable. And if, today, comfort and security were to take the edge off our commitment, the message from Laodicea is that Christ remains faithful. Even then, he will not give up on us. He will draw near, to kindle again the flame of our faith and to set us back on right paths, in his company and love.

Prayer

Lord Jesus Christ, if I become too confident and contented in myself, turn me afresh to you and to my neighbour; teach me humility and touch my life with your restoring love.

Weeping and waste

Are you my mother?

Revelation began with seven cities. It ends with two—'the great Babylon' of chapters 17 and 18, and the new Jerusalem in chapters 21 and 22. The picture of the new Jerusalem takes two Old Testament ideas—Jerusalem as the mother city of the faithful, and God's people as his bride—and re-mints them as a promise to the renewed Israel that is the Church. This is a picture of wholeness, purpose and hope.

But Babylon's relationships have been a pretence, a shallow purchase rather than true belonging and love (v. 3). The sorry figure of chapter 18 is a parody of the goddess Roma. She represented the glory and awe of Rome, sitting proud and secure over all her dominions (v. 7), an empire inviting her people's worship. Yet Revelation looks on empire-worship as a sham.

Removing the disguise

Rome had conquered the Mediterranean. She ruled from Syria to Gibraltar, and from Britain to the Nile. She devoured the produce of the nations like a giant economic vortex (vv. 11–13). In return she offered status and wealth to a few people in the provinces, to the 'kings of the earth' and the merchants (v. 3), as a reward for bringing her the riches of their lands. Asia Minor had enough resources to feed her own people; yet basic foods were becoming expensive as effort was put into producing luxuries for export. So when the great men of the province worshipped in imperial temples, John looked on this as a degrading and shallow affair. They were deceived and spellbound (v. 23). Rome wove the myth of her grandeur, but she had stolen the integrity of the nations.

Revelation is a book of warning. John urges the Christians of his churches to keep clear of the empire-worship which was such a growth industry in this period. Their home cities may have fallen for the Roman myth, but only Christ is worthy of the Church's praise. Chapter 18 is an unmasking of the monster behind the myth, a monster that John believes will ultimately perish. Slowly but surely the mills of God will do their work (v. 20), and all will turn to dust.

John offers no graphic description of the wreck of the city. He surveys the groups of mourners, the kings, merchants and sailors, but he does not take us close up. That God will judge is very much our concern; how he judges is his affair. Enough to know that right will have its day.

Signpost to tragedy

Texts from many scriptures come together in Revelation. As Rome imported goods from around her empire, so this chapter gathers judgment texts from around the Old Testament—as if the greed and tyranny of all the ages had led up to this empire. There are echoes of Babylon (Isaiah 21:9 in v. 2), of Nineveh (Nahum 3:4 in v. 23), and particularly of the fall of Tyre (Ezekiel 27:30–34 in v.19).

It should have been so different. Cities are places of bright possibility, of merry music and careful crafts, of glad lights and the joining of hopeful lives (vv. 22–23). Every big community is full of potential for good. The tragedy of Revelation 18 is that many great cities have built their life on injustice and deceit, trading with the world on their own terms, shaping culture in their image, milking the planet, and silencing voices that question and answer back.

The code name 'Babylon' emphasizes the links with the Old Testament. But it also opens the text to a broader horizon, and allows the reader to think whether this picture describes anywhere closer to home. The selfishness of this chapter is still a temptation to any society strong enough to get away with it. Yet our wealth and pride count for little if they come by crushing the dignity of weaker neighbours.

What then of, 'Come out of her, my people' (v. 4)? Are we to leave the place where we live if we find it proud, materialistic or deceitful? I think the call is rather to live differently: to stand apart from the excesses, to challenge the shallowness and selfishness, to speak for dignity and truth, and to give the worship of our lives to Jesus Christ. That is the task for many city Christians. It asks of us discernment, determination and daily commitment.

Prayer

Lord, give me eyes to see, and a heart to follow your ways of justice and love.

At home with God

Choose life

Revelation is about choices. For the first readers the choice was either to go with the flow, to accept the claims of the Roman Empire, even to offer a sign of homage in the imperial temple; or they could hold their ground as Christians and stick to their confession that Jesus Christ is Lord. Cost what it might, their loyalty and lifestyle belonged to him. The two great cities at the end of the book make that choice seem very stark. Babylon (ch. 18) is the world turned in on itself, living simply by its own power and pride. Life that exploits, that serves itself and is wrapped up in itself, will surely perish, whereas the new Jerusalem is the fulfilment of everything in human life that is turned towards God and into the way of Jesus Christ. What is given to God will be taken up into his greater future.

The two cities are like two distant targets, two alternative destinations. Revelation challenges its readers: which one are you aiming for? But the cities also give two options for the pattern that city life can take now. In a host of ways we have choices: to live for the moment, for material wealth, for myths of human making; or to live by the light of Christ's cross. The new Jerusalem sits on the far horizon, both beckoning us forward in hope and directing our steps now.

New world

Several Old Testament passages shape this vision:
- First comes *Isaiah's picture* of 'a new heaven and a new earth' (v. 1, from Isaiah 65:17; see pages 54–55). This will be a city of justice and joy, where distress, disadvantage and even death will be no more, where people will be at home with God and with each other (vv. 3–4). Jerusalem shines as the 'bride of the Lamb', of Jesus Christ (vv. 2, 9). This city represents the people of Christ, ready to meet him face to face, to turn faith into sight and hope into fulfilment.

- *Ezekiel's great vision* of Jerusalem renewed is the main background to verses 10–21. The high mountain and the guide with a measuring rod (from Ezekiel 40:1–5), and the twelve gates (from 48:30–35), come from Ezekiel's picture of the holy city that nourishes the earth (see pages 52–53). But the dimensions in Revelation seem intentionally mind-blowing (v. 16): the vision reminds its readers that the purposes of God reach far beyond our capacity to visualize or understand. Suffice it to say that this city will have room for all who come. The cubical shape may be a challenge to Rome's square gridiron pattern of urban planning, as if to say that God's world has a whole new dimension. But a more likely background involves worship.
- For in *Solomon's temple* the holy of holies was cubic in shape (1 Kings 6:20; pages 24–25). Now Revelation expands the measurements far beyond their original scale: this whole city is a holy place. Here worship will not be an add-on, an occasional observance; but the city's whole life will be a meeting with God. Even the foundations of the wall recall Israel's priestly jewels (vv. 19–20, from Exodus 28:15–20). Just to enter the city is to be ushered into God's presence.

Time fulfilled

The constant repetition of the number twelve signals that Israel's history reaches its true fulfilment here. The gates carry the names of Israel's twelve tribes (v. 12), and the foundation stones those of the twelve apostles of Christ (v. 14). Through the Messiah, Jesus, God's ancient purpose finds its way home to God. And in verse 24 (see overleaf) the light of this city beckons the world: the nations and creation will be drawn in, to the place where God dwells. What is worthy and true in human culture will be completed and gathered, not tossed aside. God's purposes end not in waste but in wholeness.

So where does that leave your community and mine? Can we value justice (as in Isaiah's vision), enrich the world (Ezekiel's city), and live as a wor-shipping people (the temple symbol)? In so far as we can, we shall be preparing for God's new world, living as a colony not of Babylon but of the new Jerusalem.

Prayer

Teach us, Lord God, to shape the living of today by the hope you hold before us.

City of light and life

This last part of John's vision turns upside-down much of our experience of cities. We are used to locks and bolts, timed alarms and security codes; but John writes of open gates (v. 25). Instead of stone, asphalt and concrete, we find a crystal river and lush greenery (v. 2). There will be no lighting system; Christ will give all the vision people need (v. 23). Strangest of all, there will be no church buildings.

Light and welcome

The Old Testament passage that gleams through the last verses of chapter 21 is Isaiah 60. Jerusalem is beckoned into the light of God, to draw and gather the nations. The world will be in darkness, but she will be bright. The sun and moon will not be needed or noticed; the Lord will light the city (60:19–20). And in Revelation the scene is the same, with God's light shining in Jesus Christ. 'Its lamp is the Lamb' (21:23; 22:5).

The light in the city, by which all reality is seen and known, is Jesus—the one who stood as a Lamb bearing the marks of slaughter, crucified and yet alive (Revelation 5:6). By the cross and resurrection we see the world clearly and truly. We see the depth and passion of God's sacrificial love, binding heaven to earth; we see the power of humble service, and the cost and possibility of forgiveness. By the death and risen life of Jesus we shall know and be known.

The glory and honour of the nations will be brought in (v. 26, from Isaiah 60:11). All that has been wholesome and worthy in human living will add to the splendour of God's new city. But there is an exclusion clause: if the whole current of our lives has been against the ways of God, then the new heaven and earth will be alien territory (21:8, 27). We shall have no interest or business in being there.

Garden city

Chapter 22 recalls Ezekiel's river, bubbling and bursting with life (Ezekiel

47; see pages 52–53). Revelation re-mints Ezekiel's vision of the power of a worshipping city to bring God's renewal to the face of the earth. Scripture comes round again to its starting point, a fresh earth with rivers and good fruit (Genesis 2:10–14). We see a planet no longer weeping over human pollution and plunder, but community and creation living as one. Peace and healing come to our divisions and disputes (22:3), as the gathered nations live within God's restoring mercy.

There is 'no temple in the city' (21:22). It does not need one for it is itself a place of worship. God is there. Jesus Christ meets his people face to face, and they offer him their praise and love. And with this image of a worshipping city, we must go from the Bible back to our own streets.

Dreams and visions

The great scene at the end of Revelation tells of a God who can do more than we ask or think. We cannot create, craft, engineer or organize this kind of city life. It must in the end be God's gift, 'coming down out of heaven' (21:2). Yet we may prepare for its coming. In our own corner of God's world we may work towards this hope, as people who believe in it and aim for it. Hope is infectious: our lives, our influence, our prayers and love can help others to believe in what God is doing.

Worship is at the heart of hope. For the new Jerusalem is a place of worship. In praise we see most clearly who God is. And worship was never intended to isolate and insulate us from God's work in the world. If worship is the centre of our life, if our worship in church connects with the life of our city, then all our living in the daily bustle and busyness can be offered to God as an act of faith and praise. Then indeed there will be more of the city of God in our city, and more of our city in the city of God.

For reflection and praise

See, the home of God is among mortals.
He will dwell with them as their God:
they will be his peoples,
and God himself will be with them;
he will wipe every tear from their eyes.

Revelation 21:3

Further Reading

A number of other writers have tackled in detail issues against which I have only brushed in passing. Any of these works would take you further than I have done.

I. Coffey and others, *No Stranger in the City* (IVP-STL, 1989). Christian mission in modern cities.

J. Ellul, *The Meaning of the City* (Eerdmans, 1970; reprint Paternoster, 1997). A theological criticism of city life, from a broad biblical perspective.

R. Greenway, *Apostles to the City* (Baker, 1978). Prophets and preachers from the Bible.

L.J. Hoppe, *The Holy City: Jerusalem in the Theology of the Old Testament* (Michael Glazier, 2000).

P.W.L. Walker (ed), *Jerusalem Past and Present in the Purposes of God* (Tyndale House, 1992). A range of perspectives, biblical and modern.

P.W.L. Walker, *Jesus and the Holy City* (Eerdmans, 1996). Jerusalem in the writings of the New Testament.

B.W. Winter, *Seek the Welfare of the City* (Eerdmans, 1994). Early Christians in the cities of the Greek and Roman world.

Notes

1. Prayer adapted from M. Pawley, *Prayers for Pilgrims* (SPCK, 1991), p. 84.
2. This short sentence adapted from J. Goldingay, *Songs from a Strange Land* (IVP, 1978), p. 115.
3. Quoted from W. Brueggemann, *Using God's Resources Wisely* (WJKP, 1993), p. 34.
4. *No Stranger in the City*, p.117, from a cartoon by K. Mitchell.
5. From H.-W. Wolff, 'Studien zum Jonabuch', quoted in J. Limburg, *Jonah: Old Testament Library* (SCM Press, 1993), pp. 76f.
6. W.R. Gallagher, *Sennacherib's Campaign to Judah* (Brill, 1999), pp. 87–90.
7. Adapted from a comment on Psalm 74 in J.L. Mays, *Psalms: Interpretation* (WJKP, 1994), p. 246.
8. R. Fung, *The Isaiah Vision* (World Council of Churches, 1992).
9. Quoted from D.J.A. Clines, *Ezra, Nehemiah and Esther: New Century Bible* (Marshall Morgan and Scott, 1984), p. 146.
10. P.W.L. Walker, *Jesus and the Holy City* (Eerdmans, 1996), p. 83.
11. J.E.L. Newbigin, *Foolishness to the Greeks* (SPCK, 1986), p. 94.
12. This phrase was used often by the late Lesslie Newbigin. He explains what he means in *The Gospel in a Pluralist Society* (SPCK, 1989), chapter 13.
13. Quoted from J.B. Polhill, *Acts: New American Commentary* (Broadman Press, 1992), p. 410.
14. Translated from the German commentary by U. Wilckens, Vol 3 (Neukirchener, 1982), p. 89.

Also by John Proctor

THE PEOPLE'S BIBLE COMMENTARY

MATTHEW

The *People's Bible Commentary* (PBC) is designed for all those who want to study the scriptures in a way that will warm the heart as well as instruct the mind. The series distils the best of scholarly insights into the straightforward language and devotional emphasis of Bible reading notes. The authors come from around the world and across the Christian traditions.

Each *People's Bible Commentary* can be used on a daily basis, as an alternative or complement to Bible reading notes. Alternatively, it can be read straight through, or used as a resource book for insight into particular verses of the biblical book.

Matthew was a Jewish Christian, writing close to the time and the places where Jesus lived. He told his version of the story of Jesus' birth and life, cross and resurrection, with the aim of encouraging, challenging and stirring up the Christians he knew.

The message of Matthew's Gospel is thoroughly practical, with Jesus' teaching about lifestyle and relationships having a very prominent place. Commitment in all areas of life was clearly important to this writer. At the same time, he wrote a deeply spiritual Gospel, emphasizing how the events surrounding Jesus clearly fulfilled Old Testament prophecy about the coming Messiah, and telling of the Son of God who is 'with you always, to the end of time'.

PBC Matthew is available from your local Christian bookshop or direct from BRF using the order form on page 111.

Guidelines is a unique Bible reading resource that offers four months of in-depth study written by leading scholars. Contributors are drawn from around the world, as well as the UK, and represent a stimulating and thought-provoking breadth of Christian tradition.

Instead of the usual dated daily readings, *Guidelines* provides weekly units, broken into at least six sections, plus an introduction giving context for the passage, and a final section of points for thought and prayer. On any day you can read as many or as few sections as you wish, to fit in with work or home routine. As well as a copy of *Guidelines*, you will need a Bible. Each contributor also suggests books for further study.

Guidelines is edited by Dr Katharine Dell, a lecturer in the Faculty of Divinity at Cambridge University and Director of Studies in Theology at St Catharine's College, and the Revd Dr John Parr, a mental health advocate in Suffolk and a theological educator.

GUIDELINES SUBSCRIPTIONS

❏ I would like to give a gift subscription
 (please complete both name and address sections below)
❏ I would like to take out a subscription myself
 (complete name and address details only once)

This completed coupon should be sent with appropriate payment to BRF. Alternatively, please write to us quoting your name, address, the subscription you would like for either yourself or a friend (with their name and address), the start date and credit card number, expiry date and signature if paying by credit card.

Gift subscription name _____

Gift subscription address _____

_____ Postcode _____

Please send to the above, beginning with the next January/May/September* issue.
(* *delete as applicable*)

(please tick box)	UK	SURFACE	AIR MAIL
GUIDELINES	❏ £10.50	❏ £11.85	❏ £14.10
GUIDELINES 3-year sub	❏ £26.50		

Please complete the payment details below and send your coupon, with appropriate payment to: **BRF, First Floor, Elsfield Hall, 15–17 Elsfield Way, Oxford OX2 8FG**

Your name _____

Your address _____

_____ Postcode _____

Total enclosed £ _____ (cheques should be made payable to 'BRF')

Payment by cheque ❏ postal order ❏ Visa ❏ Mastercard ❏ Switch ❏

Card number: ☐☐☐☐ ☐☐☐☐ ☐☐☐☐ ☐☐☐☐

Expiry date of card: ☐☐☐☐ Issue number (Switch): ☐☐☐☐

Signature (essential if paying by credit/Switch card)

NB: BRF notes are also available from your local Christian bookshop. **BRF is a Registered Charity**

Also from BRF

The Challenge of Cell Church
Getting to grips with cell church values

Phil Potter

The Challenge of Cell Church is the book for all those who are puzzled but intrigued by the mention of cell church. Author Phil Potter explains how tapping into the hidden potential of small groups can help your church grow. Sharing his own experience, he covers issues including shared ministry, discipling, communication, community, evangelism, prayer and worship.

The Challenge of Cell Church is packed with practical insight for leaders who want to get involved in cell church. Each chapter includes a cell study outline for home groups and leadership teams, helping them to reflect on the life and health of their own small groups. A helpful appendix offers a range of practical ideas for growing cells.

The Challenge of Cell Church is available from your local Christian bookshop or direct from BRF using the order form on page 111.